SPEAK OUT

AWAKENING MISSION AND
DISCIPLESHIP THROUGH PRIVATE
AND PUBLIC COMMUNICATION

MIKE BREEN

Speak Out: Awakening Mission and Discipleship through Public and Private Communication
By Mike Breen

michaeljamesbreen.com
3dmpublishing.com

Cover Design: Libby Culmer
Cover Photo: Vijay Kumar, istock.com
Layout Design: Jason Zastrow

ISBN: 978-1-945455-01-8

3DM Publishing

3dmpublishing.com

To all those who have been in huddles with me over the last few years and who have graciously allowed me to share this content with them, I am very grateful. I need to mention Karen Heist and Jeff Hudgins in particular who cast their eyes over the early manuscript and gave me constructive insights and additions. Thank you.

Thank you also to all my immediate 3DM Publishing family:

- *Huge thanks go to Robert Neeley, my amazing Chief editor whose skills and expertise have been invaluable. I have enjoyed every lunch we had together while I wrestled this book to the ground.*

- *Libby Culmer for her brilliance in overseeing the final stages of the project and the design of the cover.*

- *Sam Breen for his many theological conversations and for then leading out the social media strategy.*

- *Beccy Bersic for all of her care and attention to the details and for making things simply "work better".*

- *Jason Zastrow for his enthusiasm in the challenge of layout and for getting it done.*

- *Sally, my wife, for her continual support and encouragement for this whole project from start to finish, she has brought both her perspective and her insights into it all on countless occasions usually accompanied by a cup of tea.*

Thanking everyone is of course enormously important particularly when you have a project of this scale and detail which has taken many years to complete.

But I am very aware that there may be people who have helped along the way whose contribution I have forgotten— if that is the case, please forgive me and accept my deepest thanks.

This book would not have been produced if it wasn't for the contribution of all you. You have all taken my modest offering and helped turn it into what it is now.

Many thanks,

M+

CONTENTS

PREFACE

The crowd was hot and sweaty, sticking to their plastic chairs, but they settled down in anticipation as the young, handsome preacher took to the podium. He organized his notes in front of him and began clearly and confidently reading from Scripture.

He looked around at his audience. He sighed deeply and with compassion as he began to describe the general difficulties and problems in the world as he had observed them that week. He then made his statements more personal and pertinent by talking about events happening in New York and Chicago. It was a titanic struggle. The devil was stirring a pot of terror of difficulty.

Then the preacher said, to people's surprise, that the church was no better. "It is full of jealousy and backbiting. The church, like the world, is all stirred up by the same thing."

The young preacher then leaned forward, resting on the podium with the clear intention of connecting more directly with the crowd. The crowd in response was still and silent, listening carefully. The preacher then began to describe young people that were committing their lives sacrificially for the sole purpose of God's mission.

He said, "Why couldn't we tonight as young people march under the flag of Jesus Christ. The trumpets are blowing and the band is playing. Hail to the colors. And instead of guns, let us carry Bibles. Instead of hate, let us have love. Instead of fighting, let us love our neighbors. Let us go out with love in our hearts, surrendered, disciplined, following Christ—young people aflame with the flame of Christ."

This was the turning point. Everyone who was listening knew what he was describing. They had seen and felt unrest all around them everyday. They understood and knew the themes of surrender and sacrifice. The effect of the Korean War and the long-standing effects of broken communities meant this preacher spoke to each one personally.

The preacher continued: "I am asking young men with red blood in their veins, and young women who want to go all out in this generation, to believe in something. To follow Christ. To give your life to Christ and to get up out of your seat right now. To stand and say, 'I am giving myself to Christ as best I can.'"

By now you will probably recognize the words of the remarkable preacher Dr. Billy Graham.

Billy Graham was not simply a preacher who was remarkable for his time and that generation. He is an amazing example of what it means to be a brilliant communicator who can contextualize a message for an audience and then call the listeners to a commitment on the basis of the message they hear.

This book is not about the 1958 Charlotte crusade from which the quotes you just read have been taken. It is about the world in which we live, and how each of us, whatever our context or culture, can communicate most effectively in many different environments in many different spaces with many different people of different cultures and backgrounds the message that Jesus has given us.

My work and the work of the larger 3DM movement are known for discipleship, particularly in the context of organized congregations seeking to establish discipling cultures and develop a missional mindset. This work largely has focused around establishing small discipling groups called Huddles.

But this is not the whole story.

Over the last several years, I have realized that I spent many years of ministry doing something *intuitively* but not necessarily *intentionally*, and definitely not in a repeatable manner. While this in some ways happened below the surface, it certainly played a huge factor in the success of discipleship and mission in our communities and in other communities across the world.

What was it?

Communication—especially in Christian worship, in what most of us (including the professional homeliticians) call the preaching event.

Preaching and other moments of interpersonal communication in college training sessions, Sunday school, small groups, and staff meetings played a massive role in sparking spiritual awakening in people. The discipleship that followed empowered the awakening to produce transformational and missional fruit.

Communication was a huge factor in everything.

But until recently, I had barely even considered why this was the case.

In terms of discipleship, I have spent several decades trying to crack the code of what it meant to multiply disciples in a way that was scalable and sustainable in a Western context. I spent a long time thinking through the process of discipleship and what I saw in my own ministry, studying Scripture and the early church, working with lots of other people, and coming up with a method and process of how what I had seen could be reproduced in other contexts.

The fruit that has resulted from this work, and the movement of discipleship that has emerged from it, is tangible. I have no idea how many people are in Huddles around the world now, but it runs into the multiple tens of thousands.

The attention that I paid to discipleship has been worth the effort.

Now, it's time to pay the same kind of focused attention to communication and the role it plays in awakening people to desire discipleship and mission.

And so my focus in this book is on cracking the code of how the communication of the gospel can provide a spiritual awakening, and especially how this can be done cross-culturally.

Here's the thing—the ecosystem in which discipleship to Jesus emerges is created by the proclamation of the Word—whether it happens in the preaching event or as one everyday disciple speaks to another. And though this has always been my experience, the proclamation of the Word is not anything I had particularly focused on in terms of training other people in establishing a spiritual ecosystem in which discipleship naturally emerges. I've taught my own team members and staff various things about how to preach, but I haven't focused on this as a main task.

But over the past several years, I have focused on taking what happened in worship services in Brixton and in Sheffield and in countless other places across continents through the 3DM movement—and now have attempted to move it from intuitive to intentional practice so that I can pass on what I have received.

In my Ph.D. research into this process, I've learned that there is almost nothing written on this subject of missional preaching. It's like a gaping chasm in academic research.

In other words, it's not just that I have not intentionally focused on communication that leads to an awakening of discipleship. No one really has. There is a lot of work on rhetoric (the art of persuasive speaking) and homiletics (the art of preaching), but very little on the missional significance of preaching.

The process I've been going through is one that we have trained many leaders in over the years using the Leadership Square. Basically, I am going from L4 (the level of doing things intuitively with unconscious competence) to L3 (the level of doing things with conscious competences and therefore in an explainable and repeatable way).

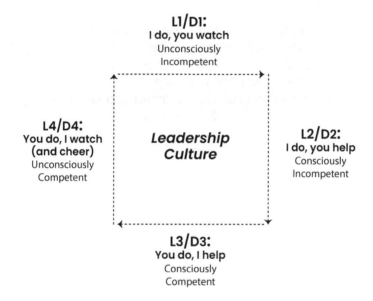

L1/D1:
I do, you watch
Unconsciously
Incompetent

L4/D4:
You do, I watch
(and cheer)
Unconsciously
Competent

Leadership
Culture

L2/D2:
I do, you help
Consciously
Incompetent

L3/D3:
You do, I help
Consciously
Competent

This book is the output of that process. My hope is that this book will explain the process of communicating the content of the gospel in a way that connects to a particular context to produce the ongoing experience of conversion.

At the end of this book, I will connect this kind of communication, and the awakening that can result from it, to the discipleship and mission principles I have been teaching others for years.

I have made a conscious effort to write this book in a way that it is accessible to everyone. And so I hope it proves helpful to preachers who communicate from the stage on a weekly basis; academics who are delving more deeply into the subject; and to normal, everyday disciples who are thinking about how their interpersonal communication can be a source of awakening in the people in their lives. Where possible, I've tried to include notes that offer more detail for those who hunger for those things. In the appendix, I have included the complete chapter I wrote for the book *Missional Disciple-Making*, so you can read the full academic application. I believe that this approach will allow this little offering to serve the most people.

This book, in many ways, is the prequel to *Building a Discipling Culture*—or, perhaps, two prequels. I'm not trying to be like George Lucas in his writing of the *Star Wars* saga, but I believe it's essential that we find a way to understand how communication begins to unlock the heart and sets the stage for discipleship to be stirred to life.

INTRODUCTION

What incites awakening?

If we think of revival as a fire, what is the awakening spark that starts the flame?

We can find an answer in history. Back in the 18th century, an English preacher named George Whitefield partnered with John and Charles Wesley to lead the Great Awakening both in England and in the American colonies. Whitefield's work as an evangelist was marked by his powerful preaching—and intentionally so. Whitefield once said, "I love those that thunder the Word."[1] The same was true of the Wesleys, Jonathan Edwards in the 18th Century; Allen, Finley, and Stone in the 19th; and Billy Graham in the 20th.

Dr. Martin Luther King Jr. used powerful communication to spark awakening about the importance of civil justice. It's no

---

1   Edward M. Panosian, "George Whitefield: The Awakener," *Faith of Our Fathers: Scenes from Church History,* edited by Mark Sidwell, 145–149 (Greenville, SC: BJU Press, 1989), http://greatawakeningdocumentary.com/items/show/33.

surprise that Mervyn A. Warren titled his book on Dr. King, *King Came Preaching: The Pulpit Power of Dr. Martin Luther King Jr.*

The title reminds us that the awakening to justice in the work Dr. King and the revivals of past centuries followed the pattern that Jesus used in his ministry. Jesus Came Preaching.[2] These examples, and most of all the example of Jesus, suggest powerfully that impactful communication is essential to lighting the spark of spiritual awakening.

So why don't we in the movement of mission talk and think more about the importance of communication in spiritual awakening?

As you know, I've spent more than two decades helping people around the world lead out in discipleship and mission. But as I look back, I can't help but ruminate on how many people who have led out the movement of discipleship and mission have embraced the effect rather than the cause. They focus on discipleship but overlook communication that so often sparks it to life.

In these reflections, I've come to believe that communication usually comes first, and the awakening that happens through communication causes the effect of passion and palpable desire for discipleship and mission.

So for me, it's time to rewind the process of discipleship by going back to understand the cause. I have spent the last few years doing this both at a personal and academic level, and now I want to share what I've learned as I've reflected on my experience and what I've seen in my studies that has so often held up a mirror to what I've experienced.

UNDERSTANDING THE CAUSE

Allow me to explain my approach to preaching this way:

---

2   Matthew 4:17

As a young preacher, I took the message that God had given me as I read the Bible, reflected, prayed, and went about my daily business. God gave me each message from my daily readings and reflections in Scriptures.

Then I tested that message against the metanarrative[3] of Scripture. I didn't always share that whole backdrop, but it was always there, and very regularly I would briefly share it during a sermon. Just ask someone who was in my congregations back in the day. I often shared great sweeping pictures from the story of the Scriptures to help people understand what God was saying to them in the particular passage we were studying.

I organized my sermons in a mimetic framework with the intention that my congregation would be able to imitate the godly characteristics I spoke out in the sermon. Imitation— what neuroscientists call "mimesis" from the Greek word—is the basis for all human learning. Recently this universally recognized human behavior has become the locus of intense debate with the introduction of the idea of the meme. This is not simply the popular artifact of culture found on the internet, as people might suppose, but a hotly contested philosophical idea. According to the described academic disciple of mimetics, a meme passes cultural information from one person to another. (Whether this is because a meme is an actual separate entity or a pattern of behaviors passed from one person to the next is the area of much debate.) What is clear is that something is being passed from one person to another, and this aids the foundational process of human learning— mimesis. For ease of communication, I'm going to use this newly introduced part of the popular lexicon.

If we speak out a meme, it transfers ideas and behavior in a easily memorable and repeatable way. At minimum, a meme is a word picture. We can see Jesus used memes all the time. Clearly these word pictures—memes—were the means by

---

3   I am using this definition for metanarrative: an overarching account or interpretation of events and circumstances that provides a pattern or structure for people's beliefs and gives meaning to their experiences. I will discuss this idea in much greater detail throughout this book.

which the gospel was transferred. This was surely true of the parables, metaphors, and images that Jesus used, and it is also true of the New Testament writers in general.

Two examples will demonstrate how this works. Think of Paul explaining his role in the Corinthians' discipleship using the meme of tending a plant:

> I planted the seed, Apollos watered it, but God has been making it grow. So neither the one who plants nor the one who waters is anything, but only God, who makes things grow. The one who plants and the one who waters have one purpose, and they will each be rewarded according to their own labor. For we are co-workers in God's service; you are God's field, God's building.[4]

Likewise, Peter gives instructions on how to disciple by using a meme of a shepherd.

> To the elders among you, I appeal as a fellow elder and a witness of Christ's sufferings who also will share in the glory to be revealed: Be shepherds of God's flock that is under your care, watching over them—not because you must, but because you are willing, as God wants you to be; not pursuing dishonest gain, but eager to serve; not lording it over those entrusted to you, but being examples to the flock. And when the Chief Shepherd appears, you will receive the crown of glory that will never fade away.[5]

I prepared my teaching and exposition and preaching in a particular way using the power of memes. I would have an introduction and a conclusion and three points—that model of sermon preparation that's so familiar to many who have done homiletics classes. I illustrated each of the three points with a

---

4   1 Corinthians 3:6-9

5   1 Peter 5:1-4

story from my own life, or maybe an illustration or parable of Scripture.

Sometimes an alliterative pattern would emerge—maybe they would all start with the same letter, or maybe the letters would spell a name. Or maybe a shape would emerge that I could use as a meme. Maybe I would say something like, "It's a bit like a semicircle formed by the swinging of a pendulum from one direction to the other."

The message tested by the metanarrative often produced this rich and colorful seedbed of meme creation. That's what many of you have come to know as the diagrams and pictograms and other tools and matrices associated with 3DM and myself over the years.

This is the starting point. But the message is just the beginning. Over the years, I realized that I needed to contextualize my message for the people to whom I was speaking. The examples and stories I used in inner city Brixton were different than those I used with a more suburban audience. As I traveled the world, I learned to contextualize things for other places in Europe or the U.S. or Canada or Australia or Nigeria or Nepal or wherever I had the opportunity to speak.

When the message God had given me was explained in a contextualized manner, the result was conversion. People were awakened to new possibilities, and they changed, often quite suddenly, and were in a place where they were eager to embrace mission and to embrace the invitation and challenge of discipleship. Often it represented a major difference in the lives of the people to whom I was speaking—and it was a pattern that was repeated over and over again.

Whether you're speaking to a congregation or in one-on-one conversations, I think all of us can communicate in this way. I think all of us can get a message that we test against the metanarrative of Scripture, and by doing that we find ourselves in this rich seedbed of creative revelation that produces memes we can share with others.

The result of this personalized, contextualized communication is a process of conversion that can best be described as awakening—the kind of awakening that creates the ecosystem where discipleship can grow and mission can thrive.

Speak Out will take you on a journey, a journey from initially understanding your own window, your own perspective, and your own testimony, to the Gospel of Jesus. We will develop a way of engaging other people in the communication of your gospel.

The journey will be from content to context to conversion.

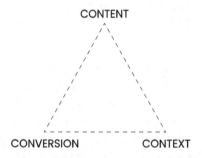

We will traverse from the revelation of the Good news of Jesus Christ to the relationship you establish with your audience (be it large or small), and finally, using the skills of the preachers in the New Testament text, I will show how you can guide your audience to a response.

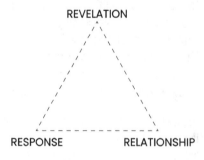

I hope you will find this journey to be both enlightening and engaging.

PART ONE
CONTENT

COMMUNICATION DASHBOARD

CONTENT	CONTEXT	CONVERSION
Message	History	Calling
Metanarrative	Biography	Challenge
Meme	Stance	Completion
REVELATION	RELATIONSHIP	RESPONSE

CONTENT | CONTEXT | CONVERSION

ONE

AWAKENING

The Spark of Awakening
My Journey through Awakening
What God Said
Awakening and Communicating

If you're a pastor, what is the goal? Is it a bigger church, or a more prominent platform, or a larger staff?

That's not why most people enter the ministry.

If you're a leader of a Huddle or of another kind of church-based community, is it to grow your group bigger or to gain a reputation as the best small-group leader or Huddle?

That's not why most people dedicate their spare time to church work.

All of us who have been stirred by Christ, who have experienced personal revival and become disciples, long for something deeper and more significant in the lives of the people we lead and serve and relate to on a daily basis.

The response that we hope emerges in our lives…
> …and among our people…
> …and in our broader community…

It's *awakening*.

Over decades of ministry, as I've worked leading congregations, leading other people's congregations, and as a leader of a movement that spread to thousands of other leaders, in many different and varied cultures, this is what I've noticed:

If the awakening that is present in the life of the leader can be extended to the people over whom that leader has influence, you will find the kind of spiritual awakening that we look and long for.

This is true of a pastor leading a church, or a leader and her Huddle, or even of an individual man or woman relating to their Person of Peace.[1]

And here's the thing—awakening actually happens in our world, right now, today.

You and I know this because we have experienced it personally. You are awake to God.

So the question is whether what is happening in your life can happen in the lives of other people?

Of course it can. It is the work that God does.

You'll say (rightly) that awakening is in the hands of a sovereign God. I absolutely believe that. I also have this assumption—there is no difference between me and anybody else.[2] So if God has awakened me, and if God has awakened you, then he wants to awaken *all* of his children. He wants to awaken all of his children to the realities of his grace, mercy, and love.

One step further: If that assumption is true, then it stands to reason that God's sovereignty in awakening his people is *already* being demonstrated. It's already happening. God is currently, right now, this minute in the process of awakening.

---

1 I discuss the Person of Peace strategy in more detail in *Building a Discipling Culture,* available at 3dmpublishing.com.

2 Galatians 3:28-29 is one example.

We want this awakening. And we need this awakening. And, thanks be to God, it is already happening all around us.

Darrell Guder wrote a book[3] that's all about how the church is always in need of conversion. I absolutely believe that. The churches for which I have been responsible have always been in the process of needing to be converted, both on the individual level and as corporate entities.

This is what awakening is. If you have a God-given dream, you need to wake up to fulfill it. All of us need to be awakened to our great need for God.

We need awakening. And God is in the business of awakening.

Every Christian longs for this kind of awakening. It is written on our hearts, because it is what God wants for us and for our world.

All of this is wonderful news that begs a question:

How does it happen?

THE SPARK OF AWAKENING

We as Christians need to learn how to take the awakening that is happening in our lives and translate it into the lives of another. This is true whether we are leaders who communicate from a platform, in a smaller setting or people who are leading families, friends or People of Peace.

Sally has led countless women in Huddles over these last few years. As you can imagine, she has beautifully simplified all the principles in this book so that people going about their busy ordinary lives can use these tools. She has taught these women to share their gospel and the gospel in grocery stores, in parking lots, to neighbors, and in boardrooms. As each woman has spoken out, on every occasion, it has created

---

3 Darrell L. Guder, *The Continuing Conversion of the Church* (Grand Rapids, MI: Eerdmans, 2000).

both awakening in the heart of the women sharing and an awakening in the person who has heard it.

These practices can be used by anyone, anywhere.

Now, that may sound a bit far fetched, but I have observed that it really is possible. To do this, we need to connect the content of our gospel with the context of our mission field to produce conversion.

Obviously, I will explain these ideas in far more detail in the pages that follow.

But first, let me recount the story of how this awakening happened for me—and how it has led to awakening for others.

MY JOURNEY THROUGH AWAKENING

I was about 15 when the first glimmerings of revelation in my own heart arose and God began to convict me that my life needed to turn around and change and embrace a new future.

Soon after that, I encountered a lady called Mrs. Demarest who was a substitute teacher in my state school in Manchester, England. She lent me a Bible, and I began to read. I read the Bible as a person who had recently compensated from the dyslexic past I had known. I read it as an immersive experience.

I immersed myself in the text of the Bible. (I found it strange years later when I discovered that Christians found it difficult to read their Bibles and pray every day. I'd been doing that long before I knew Jesus as my Savior. It was a bit of a shock to me that Christians found that difficult.)

I immersed myself in the stories of Scripture and began to imagine what it would be like to be those people. I placed myself into the position of these characters and tried...

> ...to live what they lived
> ...to breathe in what they breathed in
> ...to experience what they experienced.

What I discovered was that throughout Scriptures, from the beginning to the end, God is constantly revealing himself to the people that he wants to draw near to him.

He's constantly speaking

He's constantly acting.

He's constantly, through this spoken word and acted revelation, engaging people in a communication process.

So from the very beginning, before I knew any theology to speak of, I began to expect that God would speak to me.

WHAT GOD SAID

The first thing that I really remember him saying to me was spoken right before I became a Christian. I became a Christian by understanding the gospel, as shared with me by a young curate called John Bellum in Manchester. However, before that, I could hear God saying that he was calling me to be a missionary.

I had no idea what that was. I had visions of Victorian scenes of gentlemen with large Bibles under their arms walking in safari suits through the jungles of Africa. I really had no idea what a missionary was. I certainly didn't have any idea that *missio* and *apostolos* were really the same word, just with a different language—in other words, that being a missionary and being an apostle were pretty much the same thing.

Right there in the early days, I began to hear God calling me. Later, as I came into ordained ministry, I had an incredible revelatory experience that many of you have heard about. As I was in a hospital getting skin grafts on my legs, God said to me, "Let me do it."[4] He was showing me that the mission I was called to achieve was not something I could achieve in my own strength or by embracing my own purposes. I had to let God do it, because it would be a work of grace, a work of

---

4   You can read this entire story in chapter two of my book *Leading Kingdom Movements.*

his gift, rather than a work of my sweaty brow or my personal achievement. That changed everything. I began to see how by his grace he was able to do far more than I could ever do or imagine doing.

I can remember how, as I continued working in poor inner-city communities, God instructed me to look to the past with the simple yet enigmatic question:

What did the early church do?

It's a question that has captivated my mind for years and years. At the time, it led me to an understanding of the Person of Peace strategy. Since then, it has led me to understand many other facets of God's missional strategy throughout history.

When I arrived in Sheffield, God said to me that he wanted to call a city back to himself. Calling a city back to God was something that was very clearly articulated in the mission of St. Thomas of Sheffield and still is to this day.

Within all of these somewhat lyrical, enigmatic, and sometimes quite honestly cryptic messages from God, there was an implicit message that the walk of faith, the life of discipleship, is foundationally and fundamentally built on an understanding that God is always communicating with us and that our task is always to listen.

The foundation of the cause of the discipling culture and the missional mindset that God began to develop in me started with the fundamental understanding that I was to listen to God, and that he would speak to me. And on the basis of what I heard, I was to act.

This was the embryonic start of the things that many of you have seen and benefited from over the years. One prominent meme emerged that summarized my message: *What is God saying, and what are you going to do about it?*

The Learning Circle made this message sticky.

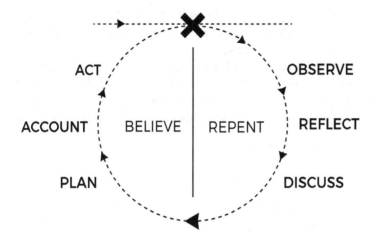

When I think about that carefully, it's clear to me that the message that I was hearing had emerged from the mystery of the relationship that God had initiated with me. It was by his sovereign decision that I came to follow him.

He did the revealing; I did the responding.

It was out of mystery and miracle that I began to encounter this call, this voice, and this activity of God that communicated to me what he wanted me to understand. The very idea of hearing God's message through mystery and miracle was unquestioned in my early years of faith, and in the years since.

As this book unfolds, we will discover how I authenticated this message and interpreted it against the metanarrative of Scripture. For now, suffice it to say that as I tested the messages that God was speaking to me through the metanarratives of Scripture, I began to sense an authentication process that gave me stability and solidity and strength of purpose.

Later, I'll show how I connected this message to the context I was speaking in. Through cultural exegesis (which means studying the culture), I was able to speak out into the particular mission field where I found myself with a message that they could grasp and understand. This made the message incredibly clear.

The clarity of this message, both for my context and for me as a communicator, led to confidence in my communication. That confidence would then equip me to proclaim courageously what I needed to say as a called representative of Jesus. A disciple of Jesus is always in the business of sharing what Jesus has been sharing with him or her. It always requires courage, whether speaking to thousands or speaking to one.

Clarity led to confidence.

Confidence led to courage.

And clarity and confidence and courage led to conviction among my hearers.

Conviction in the congregation in which I preached, conviction in the leaders I was teaching and training—a conviction that compelled people to draw near to God and hear for themselves. Conviction in my neighbors, conviction in my family.

I think all of us can do this. I believe all of us can get a message that we test against the metanarrative of Scripture, and by doing this we find ourselves in a rich seedbed of creative revelation that produces memes we can share with others. As I reflect on this in the history of the church, I find that many of the great leaders usually had a very simple and often singular message to share with the world.

I wonder what your message—set within the metanarrative of Scripture—is.

AWAKENING AND COMMUNICATION

Only in the last couple of years have I had the luxury of stepping back and reflecting deeply on the process so I can get it to the point where I can share it with others in bite-sized pieces that are able to be chewed on and assimilated.

And I am more convinced than ever of two things:

1. God is in the process of awakening people. It's not just
    for Bible stories. It happens in our lives and the lives of
    people around us right here, right now.

2. The awakening that happens in our lives doesn't have
    to stay in our lives. There are repeatable principles
    that let us take the content of awakening in our lives
    and translate it into the context of our mission fields
    to produce conversion and awakening in the lives of
    people around us.

This conversion, this awakening, is what we long for as
Christians. It is the spark that can blossom into unstoppable
infernos of discipleship that happen within families on mission,
within a house church, and within our communities.

I use a meme called the Landscape of Life to remind us of how
this happens. Eruptive moments of God's presence get our
attention. We remember the eruptions where we have seen
God's presence bubble up to the surface, and the erosions
where we have felt like our lives have been stripped away, and
the earthquakes caused by upheaval in our lives at particular
times. In all of these moments, our job as Christians is to

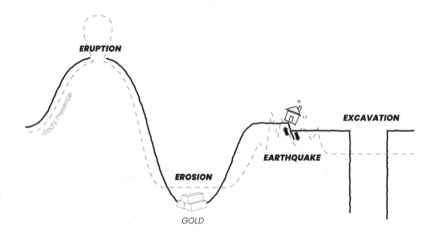

excavate--to dig and identify the message God is giving us through the awakening process: [5]

1. It starts with a message. This message is born through the gospel that God uses to transform us. Then it connects to the metanarrative of Scripture and is communicated through memes.

2. This message then moves into our context, as we connect the history of a place to the biographies of the people in that place. Then, we can take a positive or negative stance on these contexts as we communicate the message.

3. From the message and the stance, we can begin to describe the hero's journey, which is the journey of awakening. The hero becomes aware of a call, and then falls into the valley as he or she begins to acknowledge the real and difficult challenge of the call. But the hero continues, and at the completion of the journey, the hero finds awakening. [6]

So the process of awakening starts with my gospel. And your gospel.

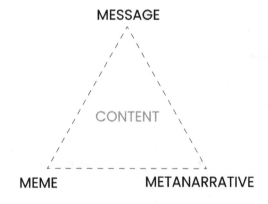

MESSAGE

CONTENT

MEME   METANARRATIVE

If it sounds a bit odd to you to think about my gospel and your gospel, and not just the gospel, I understand. But it is vital for us to understand and claim our gospel, as we will soon see in the next section of this book. Let's discover what this really means and how this way of looking at the content of our lives is the first key toward communication that leads to awakening.

TWO

MY MESSAGE

Understanding My Gospel

The first step toward communication that sparks awakening is knowing what your gospel is so that you can share it.

Now, this may sound odd or even sacrilegious to you. There is only one gospel, after all.

But there are multiple windows into the gospel—one for each of us. Each of us has a particular experience of Jesus that gives us a particular take on the Gospel—or, to say it another way, a particular window into the Gospel.

This window, this entry point, gives us access to the whole gospel. From this point we can see the entire vista of the gospel. But the way we enter it, the way we get handles on it, is unique to our experience.

We can picture it this way:

THE GOSPEL

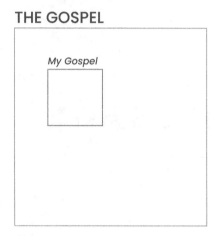

Of course, we need to ensure that our gospel is part of the one true gospel. But we can enter it in our own particular place— because those particular places are part of the overall gospel.

The idea of a particular gospel did not originate with me. Paul refers to the gospel as "my gospel" twice in Romans, and in similar ways like "our gospel" and "the gospel I preached to you."[1] In these instances, Paul is not describing a difference between his gospel and the gospel.

He's simply saying that the gospel is territory you can access form different points. Once you access it through the path that God has given you, you're then able to point out all the familiar features of the entire territory to everyone.

So your gospel and my gospel are entry points to the entire gospel.—what some would call the one true gospel. (This should relieve any thoughts of sacrilege.)

Some examples will make this clearer.

---

1   Find these examples in Romans 2:16 and 16:25, 2 Corinthians 4:3, 1 Corinthians 15:1, and 1 Timothy 2.

Maybe the path you're on is a path that says the gospel in your life begins with justice for the poor. Of course, that's a legitimate place for the gospel to start. It's not a legitimate place for the gospel to stop, but a great place for the gospel to start. And from this entry point and this pathway, you can certainly point out all the familiar features of the gospel landscape.

Maybe the gospel that you share is a gospel of God's transcendence, and the awesome bigness of God meeting with the insignificant weakness of people like us. Again, that's a great place to start. It's not a great place to finish, but it's a great place to start. So you start there, and you begin the journey across the whole landscape of the gospel, pointing out the familiar landmarks.

You may be like Paul, and your gospel is a gospel of equality between Gentiles and Jews, or between any two races of people today. What a great message of good news—that God loves all people equally. It's great a place to start, but again not a great place to finish. Paul began there, and from that path, pointed out all of the landmarks of that landscape.

These entry points cannot be where we stop in communicating the gospel. They are the windows from which we start to look at the whole vista of the entire gospel. We look to the left and see the Old Testament. We look to the right and see the New Testament. We see everything, but through our window our eyes are drawn to particular points on the landscape that are especially beautiful or memorable to us. These entry points and memorable sights make up our gospel and anchor us to the gospel as a whole. The gospel doesn't change, but each of us has a window through which we see the whole gospel.

Sometimes, our minds and hearts can be blinkered by experience, difficulty, or trouble, and that might mean we have a less fully orbed gospel. All of us can fall into this situation, and so we must be diligent about turning our heads across the entire vista to see the entire gospel. We may at times need to pay extra attention to hearing the gospels of other people, to fill out our perspectives and eliminate our blind spots.

Each of us has a way of sharing the good news based on the particular perspective God gives us on this wonderful panorama of his love for us and for the rest of humankind.

So how do we discover it?

UNDERSTANDING MY GOSPEL

Before we can speaking out using our gospel, we need to discover and understand what that entry point is. How do we do this?

We understand how God has interacted with us throughout our lives.

We look at the testimony of our lives in terms of kairos moments[2] and the landscape of life.

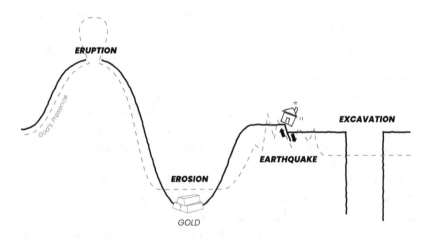

As we look back at all of these things, we begin to recognize how God has shaped us, and revealed himself to us, and spoken to us through these experiences. And in the process, we will begin to recognize intentionally what was already true

---

2   I explain kairos moments--moments when God breaks into our life to speak to us--in more detail in chapter six of *Building a Discipling Culture*.

intuitively—what our particular gospel, our particular entry point, is.

Of course, your gospel is only the starting point. We must connect our gospel, our message, to the broader metanarrative of Scripture, so we can point out all the features of the territory beyond our entry point to the gospel. Otherwise, our message just becomes us telling our testimony over and over again. Your gospel and my gospel can be more than that—if we learn to understand and connect it.

I wonder: What is your message, set within the metanarrative of Scripture?

I wonder: What is your gospel?

I wonder: What is your way into sharing the good news of Jesus?

I wonder what theme, image, phrase, or description within the Gospel comes to mind as the most consistent for you. What thought resonates as your entry point to the Gospel?

I'm sure you already have something in mind.

Now, let's see how we can connect *my gospel* to the metanarrative of Scripture—and how we see this in the pages of Scripture itself.

THREE

THE TAPESTRY OF THE MESSAGE AND THE METANARRATIVE

The Authentication Process
How this Works in Real Life
From Story to Practice

In the book *Leading Kingdom Movements*, which is a crystallization of the last learning community in the 3DM process, I point out that if you are…

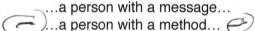

    …a person with a message…
    …a person with a method…
    …and a person embracing the miraculous…
    …then you'll inevitably find that you're leading a movement.

Finding your message, your gospel, is foundational both to evangelism and to Kingdom leadership. So it is vital that we ask the questions we are considering in this book.

In chapter 2, we began to consider what it means to have a message, a particular gospel.

For me, and for the people I observe in Scripture, a message is given through the mysterious, miraculous relationship God initiates with us in Christ Jesus, and that it comes to life as we process these kairos moments.

The message is something God will whisper to us constantly so it becomes the message of our life.

The next step as we process this message is connecting it to the metanarrative of Scripture and testing it against this thread.

What is the metanarrative of Scripture? It is the through-line that connects God's story of redemption from the first page to the last. To help this make sense to you, here are a couple of examples from some modern-day summaries of scripture.

One resource that captures the idea of metanarrative beautifully is *The Jesus Storybook Bible.* In this kid-friendly collection of Bible stories, author Sally Lloyd-Jones talks about how God loves his children with a never-stopping, never-giving-up, always and forever love, and how this love causes him to create a rescue plan after his children sin. This metanarrative is repeated in every single story recounted—the story of Rachel and Leah, and of Paul's conversion, and of Joseph, and of the Psalms. The metanarrative is so clearly highlighted that no matter what story your entry point is, you can see the connection.

Another resource, *The Story of God*, popularized by Caesar Kalinowski, delivers the metanarrative of Scripture in a story-telling style to introduce the bible.[1]

If you have been around the 3DM movement, you've probably heard us describe the Bible as a story of covenant and kingdom. I talk about how these two ideas—covenant and kingdom, or to put it another way, relationship and responsibility—form the latitude and longitude of the Bible.[2]

I'm not going to engage in theological fascism and tell you which metanarrative you should use to understand and interpret Scripture. Find one that works for you. Then, when

---

1   Caesar Kalinowski, Story of God Resouces, accessed July 9, 2019, https://www.caesarkalinowski.com/story-of-god-resources/.

2   My *Covenant and Kingdom* book and study guide are available at 3dmpublishing.com.

you talk about the Bible by describing that metanarrative, you can see the connection no matter where you enter the story.

That's what we need to do with the message of our lives. Thankfully, Scripture can help us do this. The process of receiving a message and testing it against the metanarrative is something we see in many great characters of Scripture.

You can see it in the way Moses teaches the people, especially as he calls them to remember.[3]

You can certainly see it in Jesus both implicitly and explicitly, as he captures the metanarrative of Scripture and the whole story of humanity and, in embracing it, retells it in his own life. In the Sermon on the Mount, he's clearly channeling the great story of Moses on Mount Sinai. In the Last Supper, clearly he is drawing all the strands of prophetic insight from the Passover into the present and helping his disciples understand something of enormous significance.

Stephen, when he's standing before the Sanhedrin, shares the whole metanarrative of Scripture, as he presents Jesus as the Christ.[4]

Paul does the same thing when he speaks to the synagogue at Pisidian Antioch,[5] and again (using a different metanarrative that intersects with the Biblical narrative) as he stands before the Areopagus of Athens.[6]

THE AUTHENTICATION PROCESS

I've spent quite a bit of time over the years studying theology. In the late 1970s and early '80s, I began to encounter the work of Anthony Thiselton and his idea of the two horizons[7]—that we come to understand God's word by understanding it in

---

3   Cf. Deuteronomy 8.

4   Cf. Acts 7.

5   Cf. Acts 13.

6   Cf. Acts 17.

7   Anthony Thiselton, *The Two Horizons* (Grand Rapids, MI: Eerdmans, 1980).

terms of the whole counsel of Scripture and how the word of God works within our own social context.

These two horizons of Bible and social context are the means by which we develop an interpretative framework, or a hermeneutic.

What I did in those early years—as I had done intuitively before I learned this terminology from people like Thiselton and others—is that I heard as clearly as I could what God was saying, and then I tested it against the whole story of Scripture. As I read the Bible, I tested what I sensed God was saying to me against the stories and the songs and the prophecies and the psalms and the revelations we find in Scripture.

By testing the message God had spoken to me against the metanarrative of Scripture, I began to recognize an authentication process. God was telling me to listen to him, because he was always communicating.

From the beginning of Genesis and throughout the Bible, we encounter individuals who hear from God—not in a casual way, but as God reveals himself to them in specific and significant ways:

- Abraham and Sarah
- Jacob and Esau
- Isaac and his children
- Joseph
- The mixed bag of characters we find in the Pentateuch, notably Moses and Joshua
- Debra and Gideon in the Judges
- Saul and David
- The kings and the prophets who engage in what God is saying
- The artists who create the rich tapestry of the psalms as the people of God who write their worship and their history of worship into songs they sing to God

This amazing tapestry of the metanarrative of Scripture, this story of stories (which is how metanarrative is technically defined) reveals that as we look at the Bible, what we discover is that virtually on every page, God is saying, "Listen to me."

Then we look at Jesus, who is par excellence in all of Scripture the interpretative key of what God is saying to us. He is even described as the Word. Obviously, if the incarnate Son of God is described as the Word, then clearly God is saying something significant about how to listen and what I need to listen through as I interpret what he is saying to me (and as you interpret what he is saying to you).

HOW THIS WORKS IN REAL LIFE

As these ideas have moved from intuitive to intentional in my life, I have of course had many conversations to process this idea. And the most significant ones have been with my wife Sally.

As I've talked to Sally about all this and asked her to think with me and help me understand how God brings awakening to individuals and communities, we have reflected on each of our lives and how God has done this in our lives. As we've gone back over the years we have ministered together, we've looked at the moments that have been formative in crystallizing each of our gospels.

I think it will be helpful for you to see how Sally has discovered the message of her life. As you will see, it has taken her back to painful periods where she felt deeply distressed and under pressure, but in these difficult moments she found the breakthrough that she now benefits from and that so many others benefit from too.

Sally and I have been married for more than 35 years, and from the beginning we've always seen our lives as a partnership. We've never seen our roles as positions of status. We've never placed relative value on the particular responsibilities that each of us has. In the call to serve one another and serve others, we have embraced the call of

Scripture to sacrifice and submission. We've never seen that in any way as a hierarchy within the marital relationship.

So you can imagine our surprise when, after we had been married a long time, we encountered someone who questioned and challenge our approach to marriage and life. It was a real shock to us when he expressed strong contrary opinions about Sally's contribution to the content that was already beginning to equip and inform and guide a movement of discipleship and mission around the world.

This man who joined our team clearly had sexist opinions about the role of women and specifically about Sally's role in the development of our life, our content, our message, and our team. To be honest, both of us were quite surprised. We had never seen this before in any of our team members. And so we stepped back from that and asked ourselves some basic questions.

During this time, Sally spent some time with the Lord. She didn't want to make this a big fight, and she wanted to make sure that she wasn't just harboring offense toward this man. She spoke to Jesus about it, as she always does, and came back to me and said that she really thought that this guy was operating with sexist opinions. She said that she believed if we watched him carefully, we would notice that no matter how charming he might be, it would be clear that this was the case.

I took her counsel and heeded what she said, and noticed that what she observed was absolutely correct. Not good. Yet we had a very clear sense that this person had been called to our team. So what were we to do? We had taken references and asked about this person. We had heard about his talent and his potential (and also about some character issues, which now were being reflected in the attitudes we were noticing).

So we decided on a strategy. I took on the role of one-on-one discipleship. I would immerse myself into his world, which was a male-oriented world. Through this identification, I would seek to call him to a different place and to different standards of speech and behavior. Sally would consistently and graciously challenge the views whenever she heard them.

That, for good or for ill, was what we felt was the right policy. We went forward with it and adopted various tactics and strategies to try to address this fundamental issue.

I remember that one time Sally placed him in a carload of female leaders on a long journey. He came out of that looking like he had just come out of a washing machine.

But over time there was very little real change. (It was as though his life was set on a particular course. It was really quite odd. If it hadn't been so personal, it would have been a fascinating case to us. But it was deeply personal to us and for Sally especially.)

My own male blindness didn't help, to be honest with you. We are all blinded by our own particular privilege, aren't we? Sally had to help me with my blind spots, because at times I didn't see what she saw. But as I did see it, it became clearer that I had to go on with this project. It was as though a spoiled childhood and insecure adulthood had fashioned a shell around this young man that appeared to be impenetrable to anything we offered by way of encouragement, invitation, or challenge.

We kept going with it, but after a time Sally found the whole experience debilitating and profoundly disturbing. It really felt like we weren't getting anywhere. We still felt that this young fellow was called to be part of the team—otherwise we would have clearly said goodbye to him by now. So we had to hold onto what strategies we could within this situation so as to express loving concern and a discipling heart for him. You can imagine that the experience was deeply troubling and erosive on Sally's soul.

What she said then, and as we've shared over the years and recently shared again, is that this erosive experience was the one that brought her to great clarity. She didn't expect the blessing to come out of this great difficulty. But this erosive experience led to a great breakthrough in her life. It led to her being very clear about how she could lead and who she really was.

The New Testament teaches us that this is normal. Peter reflects on the importance of salvation, saying:

> In this salvation you greatly rejoice, though now for a little while, you may have had to suffer griefs and all kinds of trials. These have come so that your faith, of greater worth than gold, which perishes though refined in the fire, may be proved genuine and may result in praise, glory, and honor when Jesus Christ is revealed.[8]

Peter is saying unequivocally that the trials we find in the difficulties of life are the very means by which our faith is exposed and purified.

Likewise, James writes: "Consider it pure joy, my brethren, whenever you face trials of many kinds, because you know that the testing of your faith develops perseverance. Perseverance must finish its work so that you may be mature and complete, not lacking in anything."[9]

The New Testament is riven through with this message that the erosive experiences of life are testing and proving and purifying the reality of our faith.

Where does faith come from? From hearing God's word.

And where does God's word come from? God's presence.

So as God's presence is exposed in our lives, his word to us is revealed.

As his word to us is revealed, our faith is founded on his word to us.

Sally found that this abrasive experience of having a person among us who regularly resorted to offensive language and

8   1 Peter 1:6

9   James 1:2

tactics was actually doing something useful. It drove her back to the Lord and caused her to ask him what he had said to her. And he was telling her that she played a massive role in the content we were creating.

The big challenge this team member brought was that she hadn't written down any of the content. That part was all down to me. Of course, I challenged that and said it was rubbish, but because of his hard shell, he never really received that idea.

But the Lord said to Sally was that words were only part of the picture. Her contribution had to do with our actions that had been fashioned in the furnace of difficulty. Our behavior was our message. It may not be articulated in clear words in her life, but had been clearly expressed in the way she had lived.

She went back and began to think about that more and more and talked to me about it. As that happened, she coined the phrase **family on mission**. What God had given us to do, and had especially given her to express and articulate, was this message of family on mission.

This was fundamental to our message, our ministry, and our mission throughout our adult lives together. This had been the message our life.

It was amazing how the clarity brought real confidence to Sally. This confidence led her to be more courageous in the face of this attack on her gender. So we began to think more and more about it. My particular specialization has been to take a particular word and track it through the metanarrative of Scripture. I took the whole message of family on mission through the arc of the ministry of Jesus, showing how he had done it.

But Sally was the anchor of this message. This was her message, her gospel, her word. As she shared it, she realized that so often women across the church and across society had felt disempowered because they had been subject to similar messages to the ones she had received from the individual on our team.

t the awakening call that has been heard by so
ıce family on mission as the final flowering of
. ommunity movement across the world, which
. _en received so well by so many. She pressed into what
it must be like for women who feel so pressed down by this
inherent sexism that's all around and so pervasive. Now, she
has taken ownership of the *Family on Mission* book we have
produced,[10] and she created Stand to encourage and equip
and empower women within the movement.

My encouragement is always to use the spiritual disciplines of
the Christian life and excavate God's presence. In excavating
God's presence, you clarify what he is saying. This has
happened very clearly for Sally as she heard Jesus speaking
to her. She shared these words with great passion, great
clarity, and great courage. As she has, she has been a credit
to herself and to the rest of us. In the midst of the trial and the
difficulty, a wonderful thing happened—the emergence of an
awakening word.[11]

FROM STORY TO PRACTICE

You can start to see the progression that we have been talking
about in this story. We listen to what God is saying to us
(our gospel), and then we authenticate this message against
the metanarrative of Scripture and find examples in the Old
Testament and the New Testament. But how do we move this
message out to others? That's where memes come in.

---

10   The second edition of this book is available at 3dmpublishing.com.

11   You might be wondering what happened to the young man. In the end, I found
      myself incapable of doing anything with him. By the time I saw him demeaning
      another female member of the team, I knew his time with us had to come to
      an end. So I did what I often do in those kinds of situations—I tried to find a
      gracious and generous solution. But as so often happens with disciples who
      you can't help, he ended up trying to hurt us. Surely that was true of Jesus.
      The ones who won't receive the gifts often feel it's necessary to steal. The end
      of this story has been a great sadness for me—a breakthrough that we never
      really saw.

FOUR

THE MESSAGE AS MEME

Memes in Scripture
Making Memes Work
Exemplars as Memes
Memes in Everyday Life
How Do You Make a Meme?

When you think of the word meme, your mind probably goes to a humorous picture you saw on the internet or social media. The use of meme as a description is far more prominent now than ever before because of the internet, which allows them to be spared and shared at lightning speed.

So you probably know what I mean as soon as I mention some of the most popular memes of the last decade or so:

- Distracted Boyfriend
- Crying Jordan
- Double Spider-Man
- Grumpy Cat
- Rick Roll

The internet may be like fertilizer for memes, but it didn't create them. They run far deeper than this. A meme is basically any packet of cultural information that is passed from one person to another, in any way. The scholarly idea is that in the same way genes share biological information, memes share cultural information. [1]

Memes are powerful because they are memorable. And I have found over my years of ministry that this powerful mimetic process can be put squarely at the heart of the discipling process. Through the use of memes, the person being discipled clearly is able to share in what another feels and does, in what it is like to be that person. Memes empower imitation, which is the goal of any discipler attempting to pass on what he or she has experienced as they follow Christ.

I have used memes throughout my ministry. You've already seen some of them in this book:

- The square (which is one of several LifeShapes I have developed as memes)
- The spiritual landscape (eruption, erosion, earthquake, excavation)

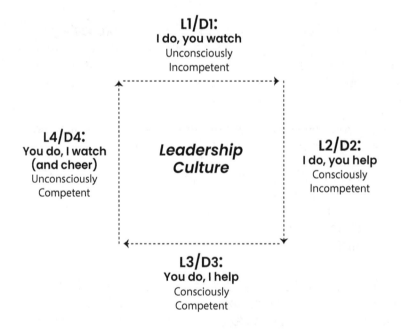

L1/D1:
I do, you watch
Unconsciously
Incompetent

L4/D4:
You do, I watch
(and cheer)
Unconsciously
Competent

*Leadership
Culture*

L2/D2:
I do, you help
Consciously
Incompetent

L3/D3:
You do, I help
Consciously
Competent

---

1   I have focused much of my Ph.D. research on this topic. The appendix includes the most pertinent pieces of my scholarly research on the subject.

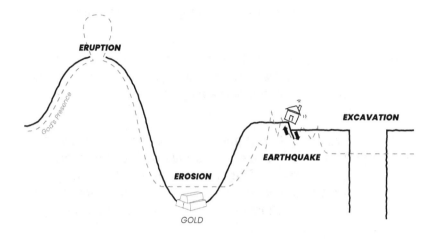

These memes are just the tip of the iceberg

At first, I did these as part of my communication, and I kept doing it because it worked. The academic research I have done in the last few years has given me more context as to why it has worked, reinforcing the principles that are at the heart of the movement.

I believe that any of us who have been given a message need to learn to teach and communicate using memes—because communicating in a mimetic way helps people remember what we're saying. The good news is that it's quite simple to do. It's just hard to learn because it requires a certain amount of discipline.

MEMES IN SCRIPTURE

The Bible is full of memes. Again and again, characters like Peter and Paul, at the moment of their confession and conviction and conversion, receive from Jesus a special calling and crafting of their lives. They unfold that message of their lives by interpreting it against the backdrop of the metanarrative of Scripture. And then they develop memes that help them communicate the gospel that has been given to them.

Peter always referred to builder metaphors and metaphors of rocks and stones. [2] Not a surprise from a person whom Jesus named "Rock" and called the stone upon which the church would be built.[3]

Paul always refers to Christ and his people as his body, with Christ as the head.[4] This is so illustrative of Paul's conversion experience on the road to Damascus, where Jesus said that as Saul is persecuting Jesus, he is actually hurting Jesus. I'm sure that led Paul to reflect on what it meant to be so deeply connected to the people who bear his name.

So Paul used the meme of the body of Christ.[5] Peter used the meme of the household of God—the house that's being built with living stones. It is one gospel, but it is communicated through the individual message Peter and Paul each received from Jesus himself.

It's the same process for you and me.

MAKING MEMES WORK

As a young preacher, I used to take the message that God had given me as I read the Bible, reflected, prayed, and went about my daily business. God gave me a message from my daily readings and reflections in Scriptures, and I tested this message against the metanarrative of Scripture. I didn't always share that whole backdrop, but it was always there, and very regularly I would share it, as many who were in those congregations can attest. I often brought great sweeping pictures from the story of the Scriptures to help people understand what God was saying to them.

---

2   For example: 1 Peter 2:4-8.

3   Matthew 16:18

4   For example: Ephesians 4:15-16.

5   Cf. 1 Corinthians 12.

Then I organized my sermons in a mimetic framework. That meme is often presented as a word picture. Jesus used memes all the time in the word pictures of the parables.

I prepared my teaching and exposition and preaching with an introduction and a conclusion and three points. I illustrated each point with a story from my own life, or maybe an illustration or parable of Scripture. And at times, a shape would emerge that I could develop into a memorable image.

As I shared these mimetic pictures, these memes were passed on virally, just like they are on the internet. The message tested by the metanarrative often produced this rich and colorful process of meme creation.

EXEMPLARS AS MEMES

There is a specific kind of mimetic picture based on people called mimetic exemplars. There are three basic kinds:

- Biblical examples
- Other people from history or the contemporary world
- Yourself

The Biblical examples obviously are all the different women and men of Scripture who are the great heroes of the faith. Principally of course you have Jesus—the perfect example that you can follow, imitate, and pattern your life on.

Then there are all these others—people we may have heard of, people we find interesting in history or in the contemporary world. They may or may not offer a perfect example. In fact, they may offer a negative example. It may be that you say, "You know, this person does X, Y, Z, and that's obviously nothing like what we as Christians want to do."

Jesus is only a positive example, but with characters of the Bible, you can take the things they did in their life and say these are good people, but they didn't offer a good example on this occasion.

You can talk about Gideon being afraid. You can talk about David's violence in his pursuit of Bathsheba. You can talk about Peter's denial of Jesus. And so on. There are a lot of different ways you can say it's not just a positive imitation or pattern.

It's also really important to have other characters from outside of the Bible, from history or the contemporary world, who offer both positive and negative examples. I often use the stories of historical figures in current movies as exemplars.

And I think it's really important in our communication to tell people how we are living this stuff out. Give people both the positive and negative of attempting to live it out. Sometimes we do well, sometimes we don't. Doing this humanizes our communication, and if we do it intentionally, it will also begin to create the context for developing an ecosystem of discipleship.

Take on this idea into your communication by offering mimetic exemplars—people who can be imitated because they offer a positive model, and people we choose not to imitate because they offer a negative example. In doing this, you will begin to create a world that people can relate to that becomes the beginnings of an emergence of an ecosystem of discipleship.

MEMES IN EVERYDAY LIFE

This idea of memes doesn't just work from the stage in the preaching event.

You can do this around the kitchen table with your children.

Beccy and Phil, our daughter and son-in-law, have a fantastic example of this. One day, when we were dropping off Jackson (their 4-year-old) at preschool, Beccy prepared to let him go into his class. She knelt down to his eye level, held his hands, and said, "Remember who you are: A child of God. Who loves you? Mum, Daddy, Jolly, Papa. What are we? Kind, respectful, helpful."

When we got back to the car, I asked, "Do you say that everyday?" to which she replied, "Of course, Dad."

She went on to explain, "There will be some day or night in the future when I can't be with him to say it in person. I want him to remember it when he is alone and fed up."

It's our family meme outlining for him truths. It ties him to his biography, history, and Bible. It made my eyes well up with tears.

You can do this in your missional community with the people you serve there.

In churches I have led, each missional community is encouraged to develop a missional statement or meme. This group welcomes the stranger. This group seeks out the lost, the least, and the lonely. You get the idea.

You can do it in your community Bible study and your discipleship group.

You can do this in your Huddle. In fact, it's enormously important that you do it in your Huddle.

And you can do it in your public speaking and preaching.

Whether you are a preacher, a Huddle leader, a parent, a discipler, or all of these, memes are the key to making the message God has given you memorable for others. They are like handles for my gospel and for your gospel, allowing it to be portable into the lives of others.

All of us can do this:

- Identify the message God has given us
- Connect the message to the metanarrative of Scripture
- Share the message in mimetic form so that people can carry it away with them

This is what it looks like to communicate *my gospel*.

We start by identifying and clarifying our message—the gospel that God has given us.

Next, we connect the message to the metanarrative of Scripture to verify it and add depth to it.

Then we create memes to give the people the ability to grasp and remember the message.

This is what it means to clarify our message or our content. Once we are clear on this, then we can move into explicating our context, to understand how the people we are reaching may be able to access the message of the gospel.

We need to know how to do this as communicators, no matter who is in our audience or what size it is. And this is where I have good news—because there is a repeatable and transferrable way to do this. We'll talk about this in the next section of the book.

But first, let's focus on the practical ways we can create memes for use in our communication.

HOW DO YOU MAKE A MEME?

How do we know if a meme we have created will actually work?

For much of my early ministry, I learned by trial and error. I tried something, saw how those whom I led responded, and then tinkered with it until it worked.

That process is all well and good, because it is better than no process at all. Eventually, you will probably find something that people latch on to.

But for us to become really good at speaking out, we need to move beyond trial and error to a repeatable and transferrable process for developing memes that are **simple, repeatable, transferrable packets of information**. We need to put the power of mimesis to work in the discipling process.

In the Huddles I lead, I have started using this tool to help leaders and communicators evaluate and refine memes. Basically, what I have done is take some of the best scholarship about memes and put them together to form a litmus test for an effective meme.

To explain this tool, I need to spend a bit of time highlighting the academic research into memes, because it is crucial in understanding how these filters came to be.

As mentioned in Appendix A, Richard Dawkins did some ground-breaking work by introducing memes in his academic work *The Selfish Gene,* published in 1989. In this seminal work, Dawkins was the first scholar to talk about how memes transmit cultural information in much the same way that genes share biological information.[6]

Dawkins uses the simple analogy of a gene to describe what a meme is like. He calls out three traits:

- Adaptability—the ability to be used in different contexts and different ways
- Longevity—the ability to stand the test of time
- Fecundity—the ability to reproduce and be fruitful

That's not the only metaphor we can use to understand memes. In the last chapter, we talked about how Jesus often used memes in the form of parables. Warren Wiersbe, the noted Biblical scholar, says that every parable is:

- A picture of God—it reveals something about God

---

6   Richard Dawkins, *The Selfish Gene*, second edition (Oxford: Oxford University Press, 1989). Since Dawkins' ground-breaking work on memes, there has been substantial academic debate about their power. The big issue is this: Are memes actual realities separate from human behavior, or are they part of human behavior? In other words, does a meme actually exist separate from the human brain? Among the leading voices embracing Dawkins' view that they do are Susan Blackmore and Dennis Dennett. This is an important ontological question, but it's beyond the scope of our discussion here. Another scholar, Limor Shifman from the Hebrew University in Jerusalem, suggests that we use the popular expression of meme (as on the internet) while leaving the other discussion to the side.

- A mirror on ourselves—it reflects something about us
- A window on the world—it is an analytical tool for understanding the world

Scholar Limor Shifman, who focuses on memes as they are found on the internet, says memes are all about three things:

- Content—Where does the idea come from?
- Form—Is it words? Pictures? A GIF?
- Stance—Is it positive or negative?

And of course, you've already seen the filters I use for a meme:

- Is it simple?
- Is it transferable?
- Is it repeatable?

These four filters can help us evaluate the effectiveness of a meme (more on that in a moment). But first, let's think through the developmental process for memes. Ian Ramsey, a theologian, philosopher, and bishop, suggested another way to create pictures of meaningful realities—models and qualifiers.

Ramsey said that if you look at the multiple models of God in the Old Testament, and then the model of God revealed in the life of Jesus, it's as though you have multiple faces of a polygon. In the Old Testament, we see God as Healer, Warrior, Shepherd, Leader, Provider, and King. All of these individually are models, and all of them qualify each other. In the New Testament, we get the revelation of Jesus, and we understand how each of these facets qualify each other.[7]

---

7   To add my two cents to this idea, I teach that the primary ways Jesus reveals God is as Father and King. The models and qualifiers lead me to this understanding. This is why I explain the DNA of the Bible using the twin threads of Covenant and Kingdom. This model is a meme that has proven helpful to people across many years. You can learn more about how this model and qualifier approach works in my book *Covenant and Kingdom: The DNA and the Bible.*

Using the model and qualifier approach, we have an inductive method for developing a meme. If you are communicating with a well-trained community with multiple models and qualifiers, you have a very sharpened and helpful process. You catalyze this process, and then you involve lots of other people—the people you are communicating with—to see if it is effective.

So now we have a filter to evaluate any meme.

- □ Does it have adaptability?
- □ Does it have longevity?
- □ Does it have fecundity?
- □ Is the content solid?
- □ Is the form understandable?
- □ Is the stance helpful?
- □ Does it share a picture of God?
- □ Does it provide a mirror on ourselves?
- □ Does it offer a window on the world?
- □ Is it simple?
- □ Is it transferable?
- □ Is it repeatable?

Think through this filter with some of the memes you remember, or some of the memes you use in your teaching and communication. Then, use this same filter as you come up with a new meme you want to bring into your communication.

Using this evaluation will help you know where your meme is working, and what you may need to add or change in order for it to powerfully communicate.

I've used this tool with my Huddles, and they've found it tremendously helpful. I hope you will as well.

PART TWO

CONTEXT

CONTENT	CONTEXT	CONVERSION
Message	History	Calling
Metanarrative	Biography	Challenge
Meme	Stance	Completion
REVELATION	**RELATIONSHIP**	**RESPONSE**

FIVE

THIN SILENCE

Learning Contextualization
Where Contextualization Begins

Over the years, there is one question that I get asked more than any other. I get the question from the people I work with daily on the teams I lead, from people in my Huddles, and from pastors who have heard me speak at hundreds of events and learning communities.

What is this singularly important question?

How is it that you can speak and share the same content in completely different contexts and the people in those contexts believe that you're addressing them personally?

How is that possible?

I can't tell you how many times leaders and people on my teams have commented to me afterward, "How did you make it possible for those people in Canada, Scotland, Nepal, Nigeria, New Zealand, wherever it is, to hear that message we've heard back home as if it's a message designed and crafted for them?"

My first instinct in answering this question is the stock answer: "Well, it's the grace of God." I tried giving that answer a couple of times, and the more mature amongst the people who had asked the questions said something like, "Obviously. Of course it's the grace. But how is the grace of God operating? What's the grace of God doing? How is the Holy Spirit working? Give us more than that, because if you just say it's the grace of God, then I'm going to away thinking I don't know any way I can do what he does."

That's not a repeatable or transferrable way of understanding the preaching event. And the big reason it's not transferable is that most communicators haven't really taken the time to understand why a message works like this. I certainly hadn't until a few years ago.

So good communicators intuitively get it right every so often, and when they do, everything seems to fall into place. You listen and ask, "What just happened? Did I get struck by lightning? Did the people eat the right meal this morning?" Then other weeks, the communication is nearly there, but it's not quite the same thing.

Very often what we do is we just attribute the results to the Holy Spirit. We begin to deflect and defer to the sovereignty of God. We say, "Well, the Lord wanted to do it this week and he didn't want to do it last week." Or whatever.

But I have come to realize that there is more to it. There is an actual skill to this kind of contextual communication. I have noticed that this intuitive understanding some communicators have is both a spiritual and a natural intuition that occurs from time to time. In some people, it occurs a lot, but even for them it is an intuitive process and not an intentional one.

And because it's not an intentional process, nobody can reproduce it. That was the case for me, certainly. As I began to look around, I realized that it was actually the case for pretty much everyone.

In fact I've heard one of the great communicators of our generation say the reason that he focuses on raising up congregational leaders rather than preachers is because he's realized that he has this one-off gift for speaking and that he has no idea how to reproduce it. I heard him say that in front of 14,000 people.

When he said that, I thought he had to be wrong. I mean, he might not know how to reproduce his intuitive gift. But it has to be reproducible, doesn't it? The basis of the Great Commission is that we teach the new disciples to do everything that Jesus has taught us to do. That's what Jesus tells his disciples to do in Matthew 28:20.

Let's think about this in more depth. If we think that certain individuals in our world are enormously gifted and anointed at communicating, how anointed and gifted was Jesus? Imagine listening to Jesus preach. Of course you'd be thinking, "I'm never going to be able to do that." Just like if you watch him healed a leper. Or if you watched him cast out a demon.

But Jesus taught his disciples how to do all of it. Then, before he ascended back to heaven, he told them, "I want you to teach those who follow you to do everything I've taught you to do." It's not me that's saying that; it's Jesus that's saying that.

The requirement set upon us as disciples, not as ministers, not as pastors, not as leaders, but as disciples, is to multiply everything that we are. That includes communication.

So when I got the question of how I did cross-cultural, contextualized communication so effectively, I knew I had to find out what I was doing and then figure out how help others do it as well. I had to move from intuitive to intentional. I had to figure out how to make it repeatable and transferable.

LEARNING CONTEXTUALIZATION

Pretty quickly I realized that I didn't have the reflective tools at hand that would get me below the surface of what is happening instinctively and intuitively in the communication process. I looked at it, thought about it, prayed about it, and took some advice. As I result, I undertook Ph.D. studies so that I would have sharper, larger, and more significant tools to answer this question.

Over the past few years, I have uncovered a lot about contextualization—in other words, about communicating my gospel to whatever my context is at any given point.

All contextualization is about is listening to another person and then learning how to say what you need to say in a way that they can hear it. Here's an example: Maybe your congregation has 200 Koreans in it, and you're thinking to yourself "I don't even know how to do this." Well, sure you do. You know how to listen to God. What we need to do is learn how to listen to the Koreans and then share what God said to us in a way they can hear it. It's very simple and yet difficult.

Remember, this is what God did for us, after all:

> The Word became flesh and made his dwelling among
> us. We have seen his glory, the glory of the one and only
> Son, who came from the Father, full of grace and truth.[1]

So many people in the missional movement have focused on that verse, interpreted that verse, translated that verse, and given all kinds of nuances and meanings to that verse. But at its very heart, it is the message of God contextualizing his communication to us as human beings. He is stepping into our world so we can understand his world. He is stepping into our world so we can hear his Word.

The Word is enfleshed in our lives—not simply the blood and skin but all of our lives, the very realities of our lives. God comes among us in the second person of the trinity. We know the Son of God as Jesus, and he dwells among us. He dwells among us temporarily as a tabernacle. He moves

---

1   John 1:14

into our neighborhood, into our world, into our lives, and he contextualizes his message to us so we understand it.

What God does for us is what we need to do for others.

WHERE CONTEXTUALIZATION BEGINS

As we think about how do to this, I am brought back to the story of Elijah. The Lord could have chosen anybody to meet with Jesus on the Mount to transfiguration, but he chose Moses and Elijah. Elijah is a fascinating character.

Elijah steps onto the stage of history by declaring that there will be a drought in the land of Israel. That drought lasts for three and a half years. In the meantime, Elijah goes to the valley and lives in a cave and is fed by ravens. Eventually, the brook dries up.

So Elijah goes to the place of Zarephath outside of the land of Israel, finds a widow there, and asks her for bread. She only has enough food to make herself and her son their last meal before they die. He tells her that if she feeds him, then she'll never run out of food. That's true, but of course then the boy gets sick and then he gets more sick and then he dies. The widow asks, "What have I done against you, man of God, that you would take my son away?" Elijah takes the boy from her arms, puts him on his bed, lays over him, and life returns to his body. She receives her son back alive in her arms again.

Elijah has experienced drought like all of the other people in Israel. He's known the upheaval of loss and grief. It's at this point that he says to Obadiah, the servant of Ahab, "Tell the king to gather the prophets of Baal and Asura." So they come to Mount Carmel, and you know the story. Elijah taunts the prophets of Baal, saying "Maybe Baal is in the bathroom. Maybe he's indisposed." Then he prepares the altar of the Lord, places the sacrifice on it, drenches it three times, and asks the Lord to send fire.

In this great victory, the people cry out "Yahweh is God." Elijah tells Ahab to get moving because he can hear the sound of rain. Then the prophet prays seven times. Finally, his servant comes back and says, "A cloud the size of a man's hand is emerging from the ocean."

You know this story of erosion, earthquake, and eruption. Of course, that's not the end. Elijah has to run away from Queen Jezebel when she threatens to kill him, and he finds himself in Horeb. On Horeb, the Lord takes Elijah back through the experiences of his life and asks him a very simple question.

> *And he arose and ate and drank, and went in the strength of that food forty days and forty nights to Horeb, the mount of God.*
>
> *There he came to a cave and lodged in it. And behold, the word of the Lord came to him, and he said to him, "What are you doing here, Elijah?" He said, "I have been very jealous for the Lord, the God of hosts. For the people of Israel have forsaken your covenant, thrown down your altars, and killed your prophets with the sword, and I, even I only, am left, and they seek my life, to take it away." And he said, "Go out and stand on the mount before the Lord." And behold, the Lord passed by, and a great and strong wind tore the mountains and broke in pieces the rocks before the Lord, but the Lord was not in the wind. And after the wind an earthquake, but the Lord was not in the earthquake. And after the earthquake a fire, but the Lord was not in the fire. And after the fire the sound of a low whisper. And when Elijah heard it, he wrapped his face in his cloak and went out and stood at the entrance of the cave. And behold, there came a voice to him and said, "What are you doing here, Elijah?" He said, "I have been very jealous for the Lord, the God of hosts. For the people of Israel have forsaken your covenant, thrown down your altars, and killed your prophets with the sword, and I, even I only, am left, and they seek my life, to take it away." And the Lord said to him, "Go, return on your way to the wilderness of Damascus. And when you arrive, you shall anoint Hazael to be king over Syria. And*

Jehu the son of Nimshi you shall anoint to be king over Israel, and Elisha the son of Shaphat of Abel-meholah you shall anoint to be prophet in your place. And the one who escapes from the sword of Hazael shall Jehu put to death, and the one who escapes from the sword of Jehu shall Elisha put to death. Yet I will leave seven thousand in Israel, all the knees that have not bowed to Baal, and every mouth that has not kissed him." [2]

This was Elijah's moment of excavation, and it became a kairos moment after which Elijah took what he had learned and experienced and made it repeatable and transferrable. Elijah was sent back to reproduce himself and make a disciple, Elisha. You only need to make one disciple.

But to do that, Elijah had to be clear. Clarity led to confidence. Elijah lacked enormous amounts of confidence, but the clarity he gained during this moment of excavation led to confidence that finally shaped itself into courage. Elijah had lost all his courage before this moment. But after this, it's back.

What was it that was clear that Elijah the prophet, the symbol of prophecy, and the whole of the Old Testament needed to understand? That in the midst of every experience in life, the experience is not the issue. Instead, **the voice underneath the experience** is the issue.

In Hebrew, it's almost impossible to translate what it was that the Lord said to Elijah. It's something like this: *In the thin silence a low whisper could be heard.* It's as though in the midst of all of the different experiences that were shaping his life—the stripping back of the erosive forces of drought and all that that meant for him and his nation, and then the upheaval of loss and grief that occurred for him and the widow of Zarephath, and then the amazing outpourings of God's grace and blessing that eruptive moment on Mount Carmel—all of those experiences were leading him to the same place: that he was to listen. To put it in the mimetic language I use, he was to

---

2   1 Kings 19:8-18

excavate and dig deep for the voice of God that was beneath those experiences.

Here's the thing: When you make a disciple, the two things that you're going to teach that disciple to do are to answer these two questions: What is God saying to you, and what are you going to do about it? It's no good asking somebody what are they going to do with their lives. That question will just lead them to run around like headless chickens. A disciple is the wise person that builds their house on the rock, and a wise person listens and puts into practice.

So how do you listen? How do you hear God? What are the means and the mechanisms that God has used throughout your life to speak to you clearly? And how can you pass those on to others?

We all need an attentive ear, a listening heart, a capacity to cleave to God so that you can hear the low whisper in the thin silence. That low whisper that's addressing you now as a child—that's the very thing, the very gospel, that God wants you to share with others so that it's reproduced so that others become disciples. After all, disciples are those who hear the word and put it into practice.

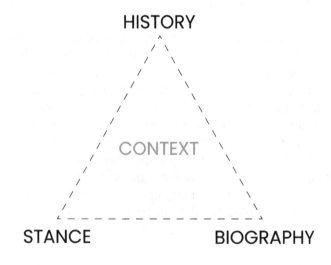

HISTORY

CONTEXT

STANCE   BIOGRAPHY

As we come to terms with our gospel, it's vital that we come to terms with how God has revealed it to us. That is the first step in learning how it is that we can multiply and share that into the lives of other people.

As we do that, we will genuinely begin to learn the lessons of contextualization, because this is where those lessons begin. So let's learn those lessons to contextualize our gospels. To do this, we will need to excavate three things:

- History
- Biography
- Stance

We will now learn how to practice contextualization in the way we communicate.

SIX

TO HELL AND BACK THROUGH HISTORY

Finding the Thread of Metanarrative
The Temptation of Borrowing Contextualization

In 1987 I went to an area in England called Brixton with Sally and our young family. We moved there from a rather nice environment of Cambridge, England. Brixton was a troubled, under-resourced, and deeply disadvantaged community on the south side of the Thames in London.

We began to engage with the community as best we knew how. We reached out with godly, generous pastoral methods. We developed worship styles we felt were more culturally appropriate, with a broader racial profile in the way they presented music and word, sacrament and symbol. We began to see a congregation develop and grow, and it was very exciting.

This was long before the years Sally and I spent in Sheffield. Brixton years were years of formation and deep reflection, and years of frustration, and to some limited degree breakthrough on the basis of that frustration. The work that many of you have heard of from Sheffield that spawned and catalyzed a movement that continues around the world came some years later in the mid 1990s.

But here we were in the late 1980s in this under-resourced community. We were seeing a little trickle of breakthrough. More and more people were beginning to come to church on Sundays, and more and more people were beginning to seek discipling relationships with Sally and myself and other members of our local missionary team.

Then catastrophe occurred. A young 14- or 15-year-old came to me and told me that one of the new members of our staff had sexually abused him. Within a couple of hours, three or four more boys came forward to tell me the same story.

Obviously, I was devastated. I became even more devastated as I worked through issues with the parents and the legal issues that surrounded this terrible matter. We went through months and months of legal evisceration with no conclusion that was in any way satisfactory.

In the midst of this, I was utterly desperate and quite depressed. (I'm sure I wasn't clinically depressed.) And I was deeply wounded by the whole situation, and wondered what God was up to.

I was wrestling with this sense that the permission (or maybe you'd call it the welcome) that we had been given by the local community was sure to be withdrawn. Doing mission or evangelism within any community requires the approval and the tacit support of the community to which you are seeking to reach out. If that is withdrawn and replaced with suspicion and judgment and even cynicism, then it's very, very hard to see breakthrough.

At that time, the organized church in Britain had largely left urban communities to their own devices. The church had not really resourced mission in inner-city areas for generations to any real degree. Most of the strength of the church, such as it was, was found in the suburbs.

So in a city like Brixton, there was by default a suspicion with institutional power that the church represented.

There was a class divide as well, and clergy like myself were positioned in different social strata than the people to whom we were seeking to reach out.

So there were all kinds of strains and difficulties to begin with in the social history of the Brixton community. And on top of that, we had this terrible state of affairs within our local church.

So my full expectation was that the local community would withdraw. People would take their children away from our church. I anticipated that the children's programs and youth programs we were running would fall into disrepair, disuse, and failure.

My own personal story felt as though it was spiraling out of control within this particular situation. I really had *no idea* what to do to continue ministry in this context.

And then came this voice—the voice of the Lord, I'm sure— asking me a simple question. So often the Lord, when he gives me my deepest and most profound insights, asks me questions instead of giving me answers.

What did the early church do?

Little did I know that this tragedy would become an entry point for my gospel and the way I shared it with the world. Little did I know that this pit was actually going to be the launching point for breakthrough. Little did I know that the answer to the question of contextualization began with social history.[1]

FINDING THE THREAD OF METANARRATIVE

My time in Brixton was years after I had done my church history studies, but I remembered that the early church

---

1 I'm going to talk about the aftermath of this incident as it related to my experience from here. Obviously, this is in no way meant to minimize the painful aftermath that the victims of sexual abuse and their families experienced. As I explain what I learned from this experience personally, I want to remember that their experience was exponentially more painful and difficult than mine.

had suffered terrible persecution. In the first few centuries, Christians had suffered state-sponsored persecution where the Caesars in their various generational forms had suggested that Christians were to be most despised...

- because they were incestuous (they talked about love between brothers and sisters in Christ
- or because they were cannibals (they ate the body and blood of their leader Jesus)
- or because they were anti-Roman (they had a King other than Caesar).

All of these half-truths were promulgated as reasons for the church to be persecuted.

So the church went through terrible times—not unremitting persecution, but seasonal, brutal persecution under different leaders like the Roman emperors Nero and Domitian.

I knew about all that, and I also knew that by the time of Constantine the estimates were that maybe 20 percent of the Roman Empire had become Christians.[2]

How was that possible during times of persecution?

There was this banner headline that the blood of the martyrs was the seed of the church, but what did that mean? In what way? How did this happen?

Of course, thanks to the work of people like Rodney Stark on the early church Christian movement, we know that it's probably nearer 50 percent of the Roman Empire that were Christians by the time of Constantine when he made the Edict of Milan in 313, which is 280-ish years after the Pentecost. In the Edict of Milan, Constantine declared that not only were Christians not to be persecuted, but also Christianity was the religion of favored status within the empire.

---

2   This estimate was the prevailing one during the 1980s when I was processing these ideas.

How could the church during those 200-plus years of persecution continue to grow to the extent of half the population of Christians? Stark is enormously helpful here, because has done an amazing job of detailing the sociological reasons of how this occurred in his book *The Rise of Christianity* and later in his magnum opus *Triumph of Christianity*.

These works have been enormously helpful in explaining **what** happened, but they left gaps when it came to **why**. Why had the early church overcome the social history of persecution to create such a successful evangelistic strategy?

My assumption was that the early church would not adopt an evangelistic strategy that was not endorsed and taught by Jesus. So my best bet was to re-read the New Testament from the point of view of this question.

What I discovered as I read is what I started calling the Person of Peace strategy. As you no doubt know if you have read *Building a Discipling Culture* or encountered any of my other work, the Person of Peace strategy is found principally in Luke 10 and expounded across the whole metanarrative of the New Testament in the life of Jesus, Paul, Peter, and many of the other ancillary figures in the Scripture.

The strategy is really all about finding the individual God has prepared by grace who likes you, listens to you, and wants to serve you, and then becomes the anchor point around which relationships are built and discipling begins to take place, until the Kingdom frontier has a fresh outpost.

I uncovered this strategy out of this specific experience in my life, and it became a crucial part of my gospel from that point on. In 1990, I gave the Person of Peace content its first public airing. I had already been teaching it to my congregation for more than year at that point. In that year, the Vineyard movement came to Britain, and I was one of the seminar speakers at a Vineyard leadership conference at Harrogate Conference Center. That was the first large public introduction of this idea.

In 1991, this idea was published in two books I wrote. One was called *Growing the Smaller Church* published by Marshall, Morgan, and Scott, and the other was *Outside In: Reaching Unchurched Teenagers Today* published by Scripture Union.[3]

This strategy was a complete revolutionary revelation for me in the latter years of the 1980s.

It completely revolutionized the way we did work in the parish.

It completely revolutionized the way I understood evangelism.

It completely revolutionized many other peoples' views on evangelism.

Today, it's probably the single-most taught strategy across the missional movement and in the various missionary societies around the world seeking to engage new fields of evangelism and mission.

By asking me the question *what did the early church do*, God was leading me to the truth that the arc of the history of the church was a single, connected reality. My experience of life and the experience of the early church were actually part of the same story—the same historical metanarrative.

The arc of social history stretched far beyond my lifetime or the 100 years or so I could relate to in my missional context. It stretched across the entirety of all that had happened since the first coming of Christ and would continue until the second coming.

At the same time, this multi-millennial metanarrative also touched on the specific social histories of given contexts. Just as it specifically spoke into the context of persecution in the days of the early church, it also spoke into the specific and unique context of Brixton.

---

3   According to my academic friends, these works appear to be the earliest date of any published account of any Person of Peace strategy. My academic friends are deeply committed to dealing with the issues of plagiarism, because it's such an important part of the academic world. So when they account the Person of Peace strategy, they usually credit me with the first published record in these works.

The history of the parish of Brixton was that it was once home to a women's prison from 1852-1882.[4] During those days, the women lived in Brixton, sometimes with their children, and the men who came through were just visitors.

My time in Brixton more than 100 years after the women's prison closed found a similar pattern. In this impoverished community, the women were still the ones who lived in Brixton, living there with their children, and the males who came through were just visitors. As a result, the children there didn't really have relationships with the males.

The Person of Peace strategy helped to bridge the gaps caused by the history of Brixton. My gospel was being connected to the arc of social history. What was happening that God was unfolding the sociological imagination for me, and I was responding on an intuitive level.

My story (or biography, as you'll see in the next chapter) of spiraling toward failure was connected to other periods of potential failure in the history of the church—especially the times when the church was being most persecuted—and was giving me the opportunity for new kinds of insight.[5]

It's worth repeating here that this pattern was happening intuitively for me back in Brixton, even as I saw the breakthrough that came from the adoption of the Person of Peace strategy. This realization, which has happened over just the past few years, has been deeply instructive. As I've spent more and more time in the academic world, it's become clearer and clearer to me that this *intuitive* process can actually become *intentional* in my life, and is capable of being crafted into sufficiently bite-sized pieces for everybody to do this.

---

4   "HM Prison Brixton," *Wikipedia,* last modified 17 May 2019, https:// en.wikipedia.org/wiki/HM_Prison_Brixton.

5   C. Wright Mills' insight is a major inspiration here. I cite him extensively moving forward but want to say here that his work helped me understand how I processed this eruptive event in my life.

Everybody is able to do the kinds of contextualization and find the kinds of missional breakthroughs that I was able to find in Brixton all those years ago.

That's important, because every context has a unique social history.

Take Greenville, South Carolina, the place where I lived the last few years. If you make a trip to the Upcountry History Museum in Greenville, you will find exhibits about the Revolutionary War battles that happened in the area, and the impact the textile industry had over the 20th century. But you will also find exhibits about slavery and the civil rights movement, as well as the rather sordid story of Richard Pearis, a colonial era settler who manipulated the Native Americans to obtain land that still bears his name (Paris Mountain). The social history of Greenville is inextricably tied to the exploitation of race, and the vestiges of that history remain in this context today, as they do in so many across the American South.

Social history includes the good, the bad, and the ugly of a context. The events, people, and places that shape social history influence each of the people within it. C. Wright Mills put it this way: "Neither the life of an individual nor the history of a society can be understood without understanding both."[6] We need this understanding—what Mills called sociological imagination—to bring our gospel into our context.

THE TEMPTATION OF BORROWING CONTEXTUALIZATION

As we reflect on how sociological imagination leads to contextualization, we must answer this vital question:

Is your default to connect your gospel to the history of the world in which you find yourself, the social history in which you

---

6   C. Wright Mills, *The Sociological Imagination* (Oxford: Oxford University Press, 1959), page ii.

find yourself, and the arc and history of the church? Or is it to look at other people's successes in other contexts?

I think the common thing for all of us to do is to look at another person's successes in other contexts, ask them how they did it, and then adopt their methodology as best we know how. We borrow their form of contextualization, to put it succinctly. But sometimes that's done in a way that unwittingly disconnects us from any methodological approach that would properly be understood as biblical or Christo-centric.

Take the Healing Rooms movement as an example. I love what John Lake did, love the prophetic stance that he had, and think that it's amazing that his particular gift was so powerfully present in the work he did. But I can't find Healing Rooms or anything like the Healing Rooms as a methodology either adopted by Jesus or by the early apostles or by the early church after the close of the New Testament canon. It doesn't seem to connect to that arc of history. John Lake brought his gospel and gifting into a specific social context, and God gave breakthrough.

That's wonderful, but it's not repeatable. Generalizing and extrapolating this into other contexts as a programmatic solution to missional difficulty isn't going to work. As a model, it's fine. But it doesn't appear to operate with the same principles I'm seeking to operate with. What I'm trying to do when using history to reach a specific context is something I think you always see happening in Scripture:

When there is a moment of breakthrough, there is usually a connection to the big story (metanarrative) and the little story (social history).

Think back to the New Testament and the story of the disciples not having enough food and "borrowing" the lunch of a young lad prepared to share his food with them. This is a little story, but it connects to the metanarrative. The big story deals with the scarcity mentality of the people of God and their history of being people in the wilderness receiving manna from heaven. So Jesus is consciously connecting—certainly you see this in John's gospel—the miracle of feeding the 5,000 and the big story of the people of God born in the years of trial and difficulty in the wilderness with Moses. That's obviously what's going on.

In the same way, Jesus comes down from the mountain in Luke 6, and begins to share the Sermon on the Plain. (It's called the Sermon on the Mount in Matthew's account.) The idea is clearly reminiscent of pictures that emerge in the minds of anyone who knows the Scriptural story of Moses coming down Mount Sinai with the Law. Here is Jesus giving a new Law for a new people and a new world and a New Testament.

Likewise, at the Last Supper, when Jesus takes the bread and the wine, he's taking the story of his life right now—he was going to be offered up for them, both body and blood— and giving the disciples a way of connecting the whole metanarrative history of redemption to their story right now.

There's always this connection of the big picture and the small picture. We connect the social history up to God and the history of his people.

To put it another way, we need to practice what Mills calls sociological imagination and expand it by connecting the history of a community to the history of the community of God. This is what I'm asking you to consider.

In your frustration to see greater breakthrough, and in your desire to see more fruit, are you connecting a big story to a small story?

Are you taking your own story of struggle and frustration (your gospel), and connecting it to the story of your context, the social history that helps you understand the frustration and difficulty and joys and triumphs around you, and then connecting that story to the metanarrative of Scripture to discern the principles by which the breakthrough was produced?

Or are you adopting other people's programs and hoping for breakthrough?

SEVEN

SOCIAL IMAGINATION

Biography
Making the Connection
Personal Story and Cross-Cultural Communication
Strategy vs. Reality

BIOGRAPHY

You have a gospel God has given you to share, and you want to bring that gospel into a specific context. You have studied the context to see the history of the community and how you can connect it to the history of God's community.

The next step is to connect the arc of history to the biography of the people with whom you are communicating.

This is an area where what I've learned in my academic work has been very helpful. I've discovered how sociological imagination encompasses both the social history and the personal biography as it "engage(s) in social and cultural criticism and even moral argument."[1]

Sociological imagination starts with the larger picture of social history and connects it to the smaller picture of the particular

---

1   Christian Smith et. al., *Lost in Transition* (Oxford University Press, Oxford: 2011),18.

individuals within it. Christian Smith contends that we can better understand the larger context of American life by observing it through the smaller frame of individual lives. We are able to interpret the experience of individual Americans more completely if we observe them through the larger context of American social history.

Smith is echoing what C. Wright Mills first posited in the 1950s. Mills wrote in the exciting and unsettling *Mad Men* world of postwar America. The rapidly changing social conditions impacted everyone. Referring to what he called "earthquakes of change," Mills offered sociological imagination as a way of embracing the disruptive change, interpreting the trends it created of the day, and preparing for the future:

> The very shaping of history now outpaces the ability of men to orient themselves in accordance with cherished values. And which values? Even when they do not panic, men often sense that all the ways of feeling and thinking have collapsed and that newer beginnings are ambiguous to the point of moral stasis…
>
> What they need, and what they feel they need, is a quality of mind that will help them use information and to develop a reason in order to achieve lucid summations of what is going on in the world and of what may be happening within themselves.[2]

It is all the more remarkable is that Mills arrived at this position before the cultural earthquakes of the Monterey and Woodstock music festivals, Beatlemania, and the assassinations of John F. Kennedy and Martin Luther King Jr. He suggested this method of interpretation before there was a man on the moon, a Watergate scandal, or defeat in Vietnam. Long before the OPEC crisis, the emergence of punk or rap music, Reaganomics, or the fall of the Berlin Wall. Mills was prescient in his conclusions, and his work ensured

---

2   C. Wright Mills, *The Sociological Imagination* (Oxford University Press) 19, 21.

that the arc of collective history and the details of individual biography could be held together in scholarly observation. By recognizing the interplay between history and biography, sociological imagination arrived at the promised goal of cogent social analysis and what another branch of the social sciences (anthropology) would call a *thick description*.

Mills suggests that the sociological imagination that ties history to biography gives us the capacity,

> to shift from one perspective to another—from the political to the psychological; from the examination of a single family to comparative assessment of the national budgets of the world; from the theological school to the military establishment; from the considerations of an oil industry to studies of contemporary poetry. It is the capacity to range from the most impersonal and remote transformations to the most intimate features of the human self—and to see the relations between the two.[3]

Now you're starting to see why sociological imagination is such a powerful tool when it comes to contextualization. We can embrace the insights of Emile Durkheim and Victor Hugo, Karl Marx and Charles Dickens, Jack Kerouac and Bob Dylan, Christian Smith and Bono. Each has a valid contribution to a comprehensive sociological analysis. Each has his or her value, and by using sociological imagination we can discover how the personal story each expresses offers insight about the others.

We must learn to do this. Theologian Kevin Vanhoozer suggests that as missionaries to our culture, we cannot detach the Great Commandment from the Great Commission. In other words, in order to obey the Great Commandment as we fulfill the Great Commission, we must express our love for our neighbor by doing our best to understand his or her cultural context. "For I cannot love my neighbor unless I understand him and the cultural world he inhabits. Cultural literacy—the

---

3   *Ibid.*, 30.

ability to understand patterns and products of everyday life is thus an integral aspect of obeying the law of love."[4]

This approach is one we see Paul and Jesus use. Paul was more than happy to use his own large-scale cultural observation of Greek culture and quotes from Greek philosophers when speaking to the individuals of the City Council in Athens.[5] Jesus used both the big picture of Samaritan history and the small picture of the personal story of the woman at the well when he shared the Good News of who he was with her.[6]

MAKING THE CONNECTION

So how do we do this in a repeatable way? I've looked, and I haven't found a comprehensive approach recorded anywhere.

Andy Stanley, the well known Atlanta-area pastor, started down this road in his book *Communicating for a Change*, in which he laid out the model of how he structured his sermons in this pattern: ME-YOU-GOD-ME-WE.[7] In this example, you can see how linking the personal story of the hearers (YOU) to the gospel you want to preach (ME) leads to connection. This is important, but I believe it is important to reach a further level of communication that uses sociological imagination to tie in social history as well.[8]

So I have set to the work of creating a tool. I recently met with about 30 senior pastors and church planters as part of

---

4   Kevin Vanhoozer, *Everyday Theology* (Grand Rapids, MI: Baker Academic, 2007) 241.

5   Acts 17:16 ff.

6   John 4:1-26

7   Here you can find a brief summary: Andy Stanley, "My Formula for Preaching," https://www.preachingtoday.com/skills/themes/structure/ myformulaforpreaching.html.

8   If you listen to Andy Stanley's most current sermons, you'll hear him do this, because he frequently alludes to the social history of our day. But as of this writing, I haven't yet seen an intentional expression from Stanley or anyone else about how to make this a repeatable pattern of communication that anyone can use.

an ongoing mentoring project. I asked them to research the broader history and culture of their missional contexts and to interview unchurched or newly churched contacts to discover their personal stories.

I then asked the church leader to make connections between the historical timeline and the personal biographies of those individuals they have studied using a simplified pictorial tool cataloging major events, people, and places along an *Arc of History* and a *Crucible of Biography*.

As you discover the *Arc of History* within your context, ask the question, "What is the history of my community?" Pay attention to key events, people, and places.

As you listen to the people in your context and their *Crucible of Biography*, ask the question, "What are the stories of the people within my community?" Again, pay attention to key events, people, and places.

For an example of this exercise, see the next page as I evaluate and illustrate major events, people, and places within the history of Dayton, OH as well as the biography of young man born and raised there—all of which I plot along the *Arc of History* and *Crucible of Biography*. You will see how history has a deep and forming impact on the this person's biography. Do this within your own communities and you will discover that your audience and their history are connected. In Appendix B you will find another example as well as the space to plot out your own *Arc of History* and *Crucible of Biography*.

On every occasion this process has led to significant insights. Frankly, I'm not surprised—Mills predicted as much when he wrote,

> The sociological imagination is the most fruitful form of (this) self-consciousness. By its use men whose mentalities have swept only a series of limited orbits often come to feel as if suddenly awakened in a house with which they had only supposed themselves to be familiar. Correctly or incorrectly, they often come to feel

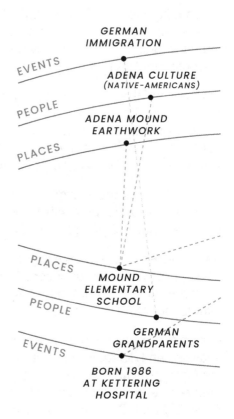

ARC OF
HISTORY

WHAT IS THE HISTORY OF MY COMMUNITY?

CRUCIBLE OF
BIOGRAPHY

WHAT ARE THE STORIES OF THE PEOPLE WITHIN MY COMMUNITY?

EVENTS

GERMAN IMMIGRATION

ADENA CULTURE (NATIVE-AMERICANS)

PEOPLE

ADENA MOUND EARTHWORK

PLACES

PLACES

MOUND ELEMENTARY SCHOOL

PEOPLE

GERMAN GRANDPARENTS

EVENTS

BORN 1986 AT KETTERING HOSPITAL

that they can now provide themselves with adequate summations, cohesive assessments, comprehensive orientations. Older decisions that once appeared sound now seem to them products of the mind unaccountably dense. Their capacity for astonishment is made lively again.[9]

Many of the pastors and church leaders whom I have been mentoring have been able to adjust the content and style of their communication, and many attest to the early signs of an increased impact in their preaching, which is very encouraging. More importantly, I believe this is a repeatable pattern than anyone communicating in any context can do.

---

9   Mills, *The Social Imagination*, 32.

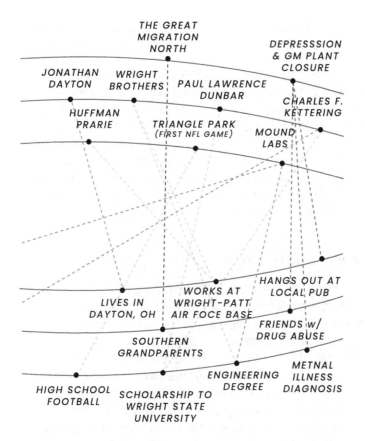

To me it seems that this way of understanding the social and cultural context, this sociological imagination is really an **apostolic imagination**: a way of seeing the world that helps us to do our mission more effectively.

Here's what it looks like practically: I usually read the local history and informally interview a few individuals to make sure that what I am saying is tailored to the biographies people to whom I was speaking. Honestly, that's what I've been doing pretty much for the entirety of my adult life—but I was doing it intuitively, not intentionally.

Recently, I was on a quick speaking trip to Regina, Canada. My first thought was that the city's name was interesting. It sounded like it was named after the queen in some way. Of course, Canada is royalist among quite a lot of the population, though not all of it. I wondered if the queen had visited there.

So when I arrived in the hotel, I Googled the location and started reading the history. I compared that history with the people I had been speaking to on the phone and by Skype. And it was interesting, because I thought I had a fresh spin on what they had asked me to talk about. I shared what I was asked to talk about, and it was as though for them this was entirely new revelation they had never encountered before. God was so gracious in using the apostolic imagination he gave me to help me to spur awakening in this audience in Regina.

I want **everybody** to be able to do this.

I've been training my mentees in this, and some have been utterly shocked. One guy in a Huddle had done the history of his context, and I instructed him to find someone whom he could ask about his personal story. After he did this, this guy told me, "Mike, when you said the biography will reflect the history of the locality in some way, that there will be connections, I thought you were completely bonkers." But when he did the biography of someone within his wider network of relationships, sure enough, even the motivations of the person reflected the history of the social context in a really fascinating and almost spooky way. It was amazing how this person's biography reflected the history. It was amazing how the significant events, people, and places of that social context now were mirrored in the story of this man's life.

The more I do this intentionally and encourage others to do the same, the more I'm convinced that this really works. So I encourage you to try it. I encourage you to become familiar with the larger history of your missional context and interview individuals within it, and then try to connect the history with the biographies. I'm sure you will come to a much deeper understanding of the place to which God has called you to be a missionary.

PERSONAL STORY AND CROSS-CULTURAL COMMUNICATION

It would be great to leave you with that challenge and send you forth with an apostolic imagination to conquer the world. But the reality is that many of us find ourselves in contexts that are changing, with personal stories that are different because they come from different social histories.

Let me explain this idea by pointing back to the Great Commission. As Jesus prepared to ascend to heaven, he gave a strategic outline of where he wanted his disciples to go next.[10] He told them to hang around and wait for the Holy Spirit. Once empowered to do the works of mission, they were to start in Jerusalem, then go to Judea, then go to Samaria, then go to the ends of the earth.

So there are four different contexts in which the witness to the gospel of Jesus is to be expressed:

1. Among the people we live with and live among who are just like us (our Jerusalem)

2. Among people who are pretty much like us (our Judea). There may be some adjustments, some social stratification, but basically we're the same kind of people. They just happen to live a little further away.

3. Among people who have some connection with us, but there is suspicion, segregation, separation, prejudice, fear, and the clash of cultures (our Samaria). This happens when we encounter people whose history we do not understand or have no knowledge of, or people we connect with who have no desire or need to connect with us. There was a long history between the Jews and Samaritans of separation, isolation, prejudice, fear—things that would cause the issues of proclamation of good news to be really stretched and put under pressure.

4. Among the ends of the earth.

---

10   Acts 1:8 ff.

Jesus says if you can reach your Jerusalem (people like you who live near you), your Judea (people who are a lot like you but don't live quite near you), and your Samaria (people who you feel quite distinct from, separate from, even fearful or prejudiced toward), then you can probably reach the entire world.

That's because the world is populated by these kinds of people—people who are like you, people who are a little different from you, and people who are a lot different from you. If you can really deal with these three kinds of people, then Jesus says go to the ends of the earth.

STRATEGY VS. REALITY

That's the strategy of Jesus, but you and I know that so often it's very difficult for us to get beyond our Jerusalem. Just look at the large churches here in America. Several of my friends serve in megachurches. Many of those churches are only able to connect with their Jerusalem and Judea. In other words, they're really only able to gather people who are like the people already there.

Even churches that have done well stepping over the frontiers and barriers and lines of color and race often find that the people who are gathered still aspire to see the American Dream fulfilled in their life. Because of this similarity, they can be communicated with in a same way—they have the same social history, and their personal story connects to it. These people are different in some ways, and so they are more like these churches' Judea rather than Jerusalem, but still the church is mainly connecting with people like the people already in their congregation.

There's a problem with that. The communities of America and Europe and all around the world are being rapidly changed by an influx of new people from many different places. That's something we can celebrate because it brings vibrancy to our lives. But it also causes a general sense of fear and intimidation. We've seen all kinds of evidence of that over the past months and years.

So we need to ask some vital questions:

- How do we break out of our Jerusalem and Judea?
- How do we connect with the Samaritans around us?
- How do we connect with the ends of the earth, even when the ends of the earth are coming to us and living as our neighbors?

As you begin to exercise apostolic imagination as part of your process of communicating with your context, remember that your context may be more multifaceted than it seems. And if it isn't multifaceted right now, it may be changing before your eyes in a rapid manner.

This is all the more reason to discover the biographies of the people around you. Find out where the connections are, and where the differences are. Unlock your apostolic imagination and the imaginations of those around you.

When you do this, you'll be ready to reach out to your context through an intentionally chosen communicative stance.

EIGHT

WHERE DO YOU STAND?

Stance
Developing Stance

STANCE

Context begins with understanding the social history and the personal story of the people to whom you're speaking. But then you have to take a position on what you've seen. You have to take a stance as you communicate.

This is a vital step in contextualized communication that leads to change in the people you're talking to. Stance answers the question of how you communicate to your context.

As we look at the Bible, we see lots of examples of how stance played a crucial role in contextualized communication.

Think about Stephen's stance toward the Sanhedrin in Acts 7. Then think about Paul's stance when he spoke in the Aeropagus in Athens in Acts 17. Both of these speeches are incredibly effective examples of communication. But they are different in terms of stance. Obviously, Paul took a positive, conciliatory stance in Athens, while Stephen's stance with the Sanhedrin was more negative and confrontational by the end.

Why did they do this? It's because they understood the social history and the personal story of the people to whom they were speaking. And they knew they had to take a particular orientation to that context to really break through with the message God had given them to tell.

Good communicators do this every week in sermons or Huddles or community groups. They contextualize. The stance may be generally positive or negative. But I have found it helpful to think through stance in more granular detail to understand why the stance comes across as positive or negative—and what distinctions a communicator should make instead of just giving a blanket confrontational or conciliatory tone. We can think about a stance toward these categories:

- Cultural Text (We can think of this as literature and popular culture)
- Linguistic Code
- Audience
- Linguistic Actors (We can call these other voices)

Let's go through each of these categories in detail by looking at Stephen's address to the Sanhedrin.

> Then the high priest asked Stephen, "Are these charges true?"
>
> To this he replied: "Brothers and fathers, listen to me! The God of glory appeared to our father Abraham while he was still in Mesopotamia, before he lived in Harran. 'Leave your country and your people,' God said, 'and go to the land I will show you.'"
>
> So he left the land of the Chaldeans and settled in Harran. After the death of his father, God sent him to this land where you are now living. He gave him no inheritance here, not even enough ground to set his foot on. But God promised him that he and his descendants after him would possess the land, even though at that time Abraham had no child. God spoke to him in this

way: 'For four hundred years your descendants will be strangers in a country not their own, and they will be enslaved and mistreated. But I will punish the nation they serve as slaves,' God said, 'and afterward they will come out of that country and worship me in this place.' Then he gave Abraham the covenant of circumcision. And Abraham became the father of Isaac and circumcised him eight days after his birth. Later Isaac became the father of Jacob, and Jacob became the father of the twelve patriarchs.

Because the patriarchs were jealous of Joseph, they sold him as a slave into Egypt. But God was with him and rescued him from all his troubles. He gave Joseph wisdom and enabled him to gain the goodwill of Pharaoh king of Egypt. So Pharaoh made him ruler over Egypt and all his palace.

Then a famine struck all Egypt and Canaan, bringing great suffering, and our ancestors could not find food. When Jacob heard that there was grain in Egypt, he sent our forefathers on their first visit. On their second visit, Joseph told his brothers who he was, and Pharaoh learned about Joseph's family. After this, Joseph sent for his father Jacob and his whole family, seventy-five in all. Then Jacob went down to Egypt, where he and our ancestors died. Their bodies were brought back to Shechem and placed in the tomb that Abraham had bought from the sons of Hamor at Shechem for a certain sum of money.

As the time drew near for God to fulfill his promise to Abraham, the number of our people in Egypt had greatly increased. Then 'a new king, to whom Joseph meant nothing, came to power in Egypt.' He dealt treacherously with our people and oppressed our ancestors by forcing them to throw out their newborn babies so that they would die.[1]

---

1   Acts 7:1-19

CULTURAL TEXT
In this example, the stance to the text is not complicated. It's certainly positive. Stephen recognizes the record of Joseph's life as a positive story of God's care for his people. This shows Stephen's positive stance toward the metanarrative of Scripture that he and the Sanhedrin shared.

This is Stephen's stance toward both the written, sacred text of the Torah, and the oral traditions found in the rabbinic writings that had become the cultural text of the people. In our day, the cultural text includes things like television and movies. When we take a stance toward the cultural text, we need to consider all of these components.

LINGUISTIC CODES
In this text, we find several examples of linguistic codes. One is the word father or fathers. Stephen also takes a positive stance toward this shared linguistic code. He talks about fathers here, and patriarchs there. Wherever that code is used, it's used with a positive stance—even when Stephen refers to the leaders of Israel.

AUDIENCE
At this point, Stephen takes a positive stance toward his audience. He calls them brothers and fathers—which means he's identifying with them as part of the same family.

OTHER VOICES
Other voices are voices that would be recognized in the context as voices of authority or influence. Some examples here are Abraham, Joseph, and Jacob. All of these other characters are viewed positively at this point.

To sum up, Stephen takes an almost entirely positive stance in the first 19 verses here. It's hard to find a negative example, until you get to how the king (who did not know Joseph) treated God's people down toward the end. But for the most part, the approach here is almost all positives with almost no negatives.

Now, let's look at the second part of the passage.

At that time Moses was born, and he was no ordinary child. For three months he was cared for by his family. When he was placed outside, Pharaoh's daughter took him and brought him up as her own son. Moses was educated in all the wisdom of the Egyptians and was powerful in speech and action.

When Moses was forty years old, he decided to visit his own people, the Israelites. He saw one of them being mistreated by an Egyptian, so he went to his defense and avenged him by killing the Egyptian. Moses thought that his own people would realize that God was using him to rescue them, but they did not. The next day Moses came upon two Israelites who were fighting. He tried to reconcile them by saying, 'Men, you are brothers; why do you want to hurt each other?'

But the man who was mistreating the other pushed Moses aside and said, 'Who made you ruler and judge over us? Are you thinking of killing me as you killed the Egyptian yesterday?' When Moses heard this, he fled to Midian, where he settled as a foreigner and had two sons.

After forty years had passed, an angel appeared to Moses in the flames of a burning bush in the desert near Mount Sinai. When he saw this, he was amazed at the sight. As he went over to get a closer look, he heard the Lord say: 'I am the God of your fathers, the God of Abraham, Isaac and Jacob.' Moses trembled with fear and did not dare to look.

Then the Lord said to him, 'Take off your sandals, for the place where you are standing is holy ground. I have indeed seen the oppression of my people in Egypt. I have heard their groaning and have come down to set them free. Now come, I will send you back to Egypt.'

This is the same Moses they had rejected with the words, 'Who made you ruler and judge?' He was sent to be their ruler and deliverer by God himself, through the angel who appeared to him in the bush. He led them out of Egypt and performed wonders and signs in Egypt, at the Red Sea and for forty years in the wilderness.

This is the Moses who told the Israelites, 'God will raise up for you a prophet like me from your own people.' He was in the assembly in the wilderness, with the angel who spoke to him on Mount Sinai, and with our ancestors; and he received living words to pass on to us.²

CULTURAL TEXT
Again, Stephen is positive toward the text here. The text is authoritative, with no doubts about its authority.

LINGUISTIC CODES
Stephen uses the language of ruler and judge positively, affirming that rulers and judges (like the people to whom he is speaking) are necessary. He even calls Moses a ruler who delivered Israel. This is another example of a positive stance.

AUDIENCE
Stephen continues to take a positive stance toward his audience here. He affirms the need for rulers and judges. He affirms their way of describing the world.

OTHER VOICES
The voice of God is brought in here, and of course Stephen takes a positive stance toward it. And Stephen also talks about the voices of the slaves in Egypt, and takes a negative stance toward their approach to Moses.

---

2   Acts 7:20-38

It's important to note here that we usually think of Stephen's address toward the Sanhedrin as negative. We imagine the paint peeling off the walls from his rhetoric. But we're more than halfway in here, and the stance is overwhelming positive. We're not to the hammer blow yet.

This is something we as communicators need to consider—the value of starting a message with a positive stance.

Let's move on to the next section.

> But our ancestors refused to obey him. Instead,
> they rejected him and in their hearts turned back to
> Egypt. They told Aaron, 'Make us gods who will go
> before us. As for this fellow Moses who led us out of
> Egypt—we don't know what has happened to him!'
> That was the time they made an idol in the form of a
> calf. They brought sacrifices to it and reveled in what
> their own hands had made. But God turned away from
> them and gave them over to the worship of the sun,
> moon and stars. This agrees with what is written in the
> book of the prophets:
>
> Did you bring me sacrifices and offerings
>   forty years in the wilderness, people of Israel?
> You have taken up the tabernacle of Molek
>   and the star of your god Rephan,
>   the idols you made to worship.
> Therefore I will send you into exile beyond Babylon.
>
> Our ancestors had the tabernacle of the covenant
> law with them in the wilderness. It had been made as
> God directed Moses, according to the pattern he had
> seen. After receiving the tabernacle, our ancestors under
> Joshua brought it with them when they took the land
> from the nations God drove out before them. It remained
> in the land until the time of David, who enjoyed God's
> favor and asked that he might provide a dwelling place
> for the God of Jacob. But it was Solomon who built a
> house for him.

However, the Most High does not live in houses made by human hands. As the prophet says:

'Heaven is my throne,
    and the earth is my footstool.
What kind of house will you build for me?'
    says the Lord.
'Or where will my resting place be?
    Has not my hand made all these things?' [3]

In this section, we can say in general that we have a continuing positive stance toward text and continuing positive stance toward linguistic codes, because Stephen is still using the same language.

But when it comes to other voices and audience, something else is starting to pick up. We see Stephen discussing how our fathers refused to obey and rejected Moses. Their hearts were turned to Egypt, and they asked Aaron to make gods for them. Stephen treats these voices in the wilderness with a negative stance.

Even the way Stephen describes Moses is turning. Moses is "this fellow," instead of brother or prophet. This is a turn toward a negative stance.

Now let's look at how Stephen treats his audience. Initially, there was identification, but here comes the differentiation. This differentiation is important, because it sets Stephen up to challenge his audience. [4]

Remember, Stephen was charged with continually speaking "against this holy place and against the law." [5] So as his stance becomes challenging to his audience, he tells his accusers

---

3   Acts 7:39-50

4   If you've heard or read my teaching about invitation and challenge, this will make sense. This approach is woven into the DNA of the Bible—God starts by identifying with us by extending a covenant relationship to his people.

5   Acts 6:13. Stephen was even called "this fellow" in the charge. As I just mentioned, Stephen used the same language to refer to Moses in this section of the text.

that "the Most High does not live in houses made by human hands."[6] Stephen is basically heading in a direction that suggests that things made with human hands—even the Temple—had become idols. Examining the stance helps us see how Stephen is directly challenging his audience here— telling them that they are honoring the Temple above even their relationship with God.

As we look back through the stance of Stephen's message, we see he is saying that Jesus is like Moses. From the very beginning, there was a division among the people as to whether to accept the God-given ruler who is the King, the God-given Judge, and Deliverer. This is further articulated in the separation of the people at Mt. Sinai. A whole bunch of people there were not really interested in Moses anymore. They were interested in something they could make with their own hands as a means of sacrificial worship.

This division is expounded by the prophets who say that heaven is God's throne. There's kind of growing differentiation in the audience because a group of people doesn't accept God's given ruler and is prepared to wait on the word of God. Instead, this group—which the Sanhedrin was a part of—was much more keen to start creating gods after their own image.

Analyzing the stance helps us see how much Stephen is challenging the Sanhedrin. So we shouldn't be surprised at what happens here at the end of the passage.

> "You stiff-necked people! Your hearts and ears are still uncircumcised. You are just like your ancestors: You always resist the Holy Spirit! Was there ever a prophet your ancestors did not persecute? They even killed those who predicted the coming of the Righteous One. And now you have betrayed and murdered him—you who have received the law that was given through angels but have not obeyed it." [7]

---

6   Acts 7:48

7   Acts 7:50-53

Not much doubt about the stance here. While Stephen still affirms the common cultural text, he changes the way he is using linguistic codes by saying things like "your ancestors." In other words, the language is showing that Stephen's fathers—the patriarchs Abraham and Moses—are in one camp, while the Sanhedrin's ancestors are the people who asked Aaron for a golden calf and those who persecuted the prophets. And it's clear that Stephen's stance toward his audience is starkly negative—"you stiff-necked people" is confrontation, not conciliation.

Make sure you see how Stephen gets to this point. He does it by using overwhelming positive stance at the beginning and then beginning to introduce a negative stance. My guess is that he does this so as to judge the response in the audience to see whether there's any chance of them coming over onto his side. That is the way I would do it if I were in that situation. Your overwhelmingly positive stance provides a hearing amongst your audience, but nobody listens if you start out negatively.

Even with this most confrontational of sermons, it's interesting how positive Stephen is in general in relation to the main components of the communicative process. He has no liberty to be anything other than positive about their cultural text. He shares that with the Sanhedrin. For the most part, he is positive about the linguistic codes.

He starts out specifically positive toward the audience and the other voices but begins to weave in a negative stance so as to give the opportunity to his audience to come with him. Not all of them do. So the stance turns more and more negative as Stephen brings challenge.

This is an important lesson about communicative stance for us to take to heart. After all, we want the maximum number of people listening to our message, to our gospel. You need to start by identification, which happens via a positive stance. This is an invitational approach.

Here's a modern-day example: if you are speaking in the south in the United States, you can't communicate starting with a negative stance toward the Civil War. You may get there eventually, but you can't start there. Our stance or posture toward an individual in one-on-one conversation is just as important.

What the best communicators in the Bible do in terms of stance is seek to gain an audience and then move that audience toward Jesus through discipleship. How do they do this? By developing a positive stance toward text, linguistic codes, audience, and other voices.

Of course, you can't do this with a blanket statement. When Paul spoke in Athens in Acts 17, he had to be selective about the other voices he mentioned. Some he simply didn't bring up.

But what we find as we study communicative stance in the book of Acts is that the best communicators find ways to create a general attitude of positivity that allows your audience to be awakened in the way that you're looking for.[8] We never develop a negative stance toward an audience to start, nor should we take an overly negative stance in other places. This is part of what it takes to be an effective communicator.

We need to figure out how to speak out of this kind of stance. So in the next chapter, we will look at Paul and Peter and how they communicated in the book of Acts to see what we can learn about developing a communicative stance.

---

8   This is definitely not the way that most evangelical Christians are operating in the public arena right now. Most of the speaking out I see does not take a positive stance toward cultural texts, linguistic codes, audience, and other voices. If you listen to daytime radio or watch certain cable TV stations or websites, you'll find people who speak effectively to existing constituencies, but who aren't winning any new audience. Frankly it shocks me that evangelicals aren't looking to develop a new audience. If we want transformation and change, we need a new audience. And if we want a new audience, we need to start with a positive stance. That identification and invitation is a bridge where the first steps of discipleship can take place. Isn't that what we all want?

DEVELOPING STANCE

In the last chapter, we went through Stephen's speech in great detail, to understand the communicative stance we used. Throughout the chapter, we alluded to Paul's message to the Athenians in Acts 17. Let's look at that now.

> While Paul was waiting for them in Athens, he was greatly distressed to see that the city was full of idols. So he reasoned in the synagogue with both Jews and God-fearing Greeks, as well as in the marketplace day by day with those who happened to be there. A group of Epicurean and Stoic philosophers began to debate with him. Some of them asked, "What is this babbler trying to say?" Others remarked, "He seems to be advocating foreign gods." They said this because Paul was preaching the good news about Jesus and the resurrection. Then they took him and brought him to a meeting of the Areopagus, where they said to him, "May we know what this new teaching is that you are presenting? You are bringing some strange ideas to our ears, and we would like to know what they mean." (All the Athenians and the foreigners who lived there spent their time doing nothing but talking about and listening to the latest ideas.)
>
> Paul then stood up in the meeting of the Areopagus and said: "People of Athens! I see that in every way you are very religious. For as I walked around and looked carefully at your objects of worship, I even found an altar with this inscription: to an unknown god. So you are ignorant of the very thing you worship—and this is what I am going to proclaim to you.
>
> The God who made the world and everything in it is the Lord of heaven and earth and does not live in temples built by human hands. And he is not served by human hands, as if he needed anything. Rather, he himself gives everyone life and breath and everything else. From one man he made all the nations, that they

should inhabit the whole earth; and he marked out their appointed times in history and the boundaries of their lands. God did this so that they would seek him and perhaps reach out for him and find him, though he is not far from any one of us. 'For in him we live and move and have our being.' As some of your own poets have said, 'We are his offspring.'

Therefore since we are God's offspring, we should not think that the divine being is like gold or silver or stone— an image made by human design and skill. In the past God overlooked such ignorance, but now he commands all people everywhere to repent. For he has set a day when he will judge the world with justice by the man he has appointed. He has given proof of this to everyone by raising him from the dead.

When they heard about the resurrection of the dead, some of them sneered, but others said, "We want to hear you again on this subject." At that, Paul left the Council. Some of the people became followers of Paul and believed. Among them was Dionysius, a member of the Areopagus, also a woman named Damaris, and a number of others.[9]

Let's break down Paul's stance using our four categories.

He shows a positive stance toward the cultural text, and especially toward the social history of Athens. Mark the places where you see this positive stance in this passage with a pound sign.

He shows a positive stance toward the linguistic code, and even calls their idolatry an act of worship. Mark the places where you see this positive stance in this passage with a star.

He shows a positive stance toward the other voices, and even quotes Epicurean and Stoic philosophers. Mark the places

---

9   Acts 17:16-34

where you see this positive stance in this passage with an asterisk.

When it comes to the audience, Paul uses both a positive and negative stance. He talks about them as children of God, but goes on to talk about their potential ignorance if they continue to worship man-made objects. Mark the places where you see these positive and negative stances with plus and minus signs.[10] If you find negative examples in the other categories, mark them as well.

Now it's your turn. Let's look at Peter's message in Acts 2 and break it down yourself.

> Then Peter stood up with the Eleven, raised his voice and addressed the crowd: "Fellow Jews and all of you who live in Jerusalem, let me explain this to you; listen carefully to what I say. These people are not drunk, as you suppose. It's only nine in the morning! No, this is what was spoken by the prophet Joel:
>
> In the last days, God says,
>   I will pour out my Spirit on all people.
> Your sons and daughters will prophesy,
>   your young men will see visions,
>   your old men will dream dreams.
> Even on my servants, both men and women,
>   I will pour out my Spirit in those days,
>   and they will prophesy.
> I will show wonders in the heavens above
>   and signs on the earth below,
>   blood and fire and billows of smoke.
> The sun will be turned to darkness
>   and the moon to blood
> before the coming of the great and glorious day of
>   the Lord.
> And everyone who calls
>   on the name of the Lord will be saved.'

---

10   Some people find it helpful to use different colors rather than different symbols when showing stance. Feel free to create a legend that works for you.

*Fellow Israelites, listen to this: Jesus of Nazareth was a
man accredited by God to you by miracles, wonders and
signs, which God did among you through him, as you
yourselves know. This man was handed over to you by
God's deliberate plan and foreknowledge; and you, with
the help of wicked men, put him to death by nailing him
to the cross. But God raised him from the dead, freeing
him from the agony of death, because it was impossible
for death to keep its hold on him. David said about him:*

I saw the Lord always before me.
  Because he is at my right hand,
I will not be shaken.
Therefore my heart is glad and my tongue rejoices;
  my body also will rest in hope,
*because you will not abandon me to the realm of the
  dead, you will not let your holy one see decay.*
You have made known to me the paths of life;
  you will fill me with joy in your presence.'

*Fellow Israelites, I can tell you confidently that the
patriarch David died and was buried, and his tomb is
here to this day. But he was a prophet and knew that
God had promised him on oath that he would place
one of his descendants on his throne. Seeing what was
to come, he spoke of the resurrection of the Messiah,
that he was not abandoned to the realm of the dead,
nor did his body see decay. God has raised this Jesus
to life, and we are all witnesses of it. Exalted to the
right hand of God, he has received from the Father the
promised Holy Spirit and has poured out what you now
see and hear. For David did not ascend to heaven, and
yet he said,*

The Lord said to my Lord:
  'Sit at my right hand
until I make your enemies
  a footstool for your feet.'

*Therefore let all Israel be assured of this: God has made
this Jesus, whom you crucified, both Lord and Messiah.*

When the people heard this, they were cut to the heart and said to Peter and the other apostles, 'Brothers, what shall we do?'

Peter replied, 'Repent and be baptized, every one of you, in the name of Jesus Christ for the forgiveness of your sins. And you will receive the gift of the Holy Spirit. The promise is for you and your children and for all who are far off—for all whom the Lord our God will call.'

With many other words he warned them; and he pleaded with them, 'Save yourselves from this corrupt generation.' Those who accepted his message were baptized, and about three thousand were added to their number that day.[11]

As a reminder, the categories are:

- Cultural Text
- Linguistic Codes
- Audience
- Other Voices

Now that you've got the hang of it, break out your most recent sermon or teaching session or paper or blog post or whatever. Do the same exercise and see what your stance is.

As you use this tool, you'll discover the power of understanding what stance you are communicating with, and you will begin to move toward identifying with your audience no matter what their context is.

And you'll be ready to move your focus onto the conversion that happens as your speaking out awakens the people who hear you.

---

11 Acts 2:14-41

PART THREE
CONVERSION

COMMUNICATION DASHBOARD

CONTENT	CONTEXT	CONVERSION
Message	History	Calling
Metanarrative	Biography	Challenge
Meme	Stance	Completion
REVELATION	RELATIONSHIP	RESPONSE

NINE

THE HERO'S JOURNEY

CONVERSION: FROM WHAT TO WHAT, AND BY WHAT MEANS?

I love movies. If I'm not watching football (what we Americans call "soccer"), then I'm probably watching the latest movie. I love watching the stories of the heroes of the cinema.

Of course, these heroes take different forms. Some find courage, like Frodo Baggins. Some find empathy, like Ebenezer Scrooge. Some find purpose, like Luke Skywalker. I'm sure you can think of countless more examples.

The hero's journey is the basic mythology of the world. It is ubiquitous across a multiplicity of cultures, and is deeply ingrained in our Western culture today. No matter what point in history you examine, you will likely find a hero's journey. It goes all the way back to Ulysses in Homer's *The Iliad* and *The Odyssey* of Ancient Greece, to the tales of Beowulf and King Arthur in the middle ages in England, all the way to the Academy Award-winning movies of today. Even anarchic writers like Ernest Hemingway and Cormac McCarthy or J.D. Salinger take their heroes on a "life" journey.

The hero's journey was perhaps first fully articulated with the work of Joseph Campbell in his book *The Hero with a Thousand Faces* being the most influential.[1] Campbell noticed that many cultures had a similar story and narrative structure that defined who their heroes and heroines were. These tales help these cultures understand the nature, purpose, and responsibilities of life.

Recently, in a conversation with our son Sam, he recommended a Netflix movie called *Dawn Wall*. It sounded like science fiction, but it is in fact a movie about the free climber Tommy Caldwell who tries to scale the Dawn Wall of El Capitan in Yosemite National Park, in a brave effort to come to terms with some tragic circumstances in his life.

It's a classic true-life, hero-to-mentor journey. It is so well worth watching. Like all the examples,

1. He is an unlikely hero. Shy and timid as a child, no particular skills.

2. He enters the specialist climbing world and overcomes difficulties all the time.

3. He then has the challenge physically and emotionally to conquer the Dawn Wall.

4. After he overcomes, he mentors and stays with his disciple to enable him to succeed too.

It is truly inspiring, even if you don't like heights.

Let's break down the journey using a well known example from the work of J.R.R. Tolkien:

- an unlikely hero (Frodo Baggins);
- enters another world (Mordor);

---

1   I also recommend Christopher Vogler's book *The Writer's Journey: Mythic Structure for Writers* and Jonah Sachs' *Winning the Story Wars* as resources about the hero's journey.

- to fulfill a great quest (destroy the Ring of Power);
- with the help of an older and wiser mentor (Gandalf).

I agree with Campbell's assertion that the hero's journey is generally[2] the primary narrative of any culture you examine.[3]

Every life doesn't go like this, but the heroic stories are the ones we retell. And when we retell them, we're giving our audience an insight (we might even say a code) into what we hope for or expect.

So understanding and using the hero's journey is a key part of Speaking Out in a manner that awakens others to discipleship and mission. I have realized that if we can put this code of the hero's journey to use, we can catalyze the process of conversion within our audiences that leads to a change in their lives that really matters.[4]

WHAT IS THE HERO'S JOURNEY?

The hero's journey is a narrative or story common to every culture around the world. It's found throughout the Bible and represents the narrative process for every heroic story of faith. It usually entails a woman or a man encountering an inciting moment of challenge, change, or crisis that takes them on a journey.

The Bible would typically represent this as a journey into an actual or metaphysical desert or the valley. (Think of the examples of Elijah and Jesus here.) In ancient mythology, it was the journey into the underworld, or maybe a journey into

---

2   Maybe this is not the case universally, but it is undoubtedly the case generally.

3   Interesting side note: Campbell consulted with George Lucas during the creation of the original *Star Wars* trilogy. No wonder Luke Skywalker (an unlikely hero) enters another world (away from Tattooine) to fulfill a great quest (defeating the Empire) with the help of an older and wiser mentor (Obi-Wan Kenobi, and then Yoda).

4   We talked about models and qualifiers in the previous section of the book. I have found the hero's journey to be one of the powerful and resonant models by which to understand the Bible.

the unreached and uncharted places as you get on a ship and travel to the horizon. (Think of Odysseus.)

This journey exposes weaknesses or potential frailties in the hero. The weaknesses that are exposed are dealt with in different ways. They either function as something of an Achilles' heel when the hero faces the antagonist in the story, or they function as a corrective when the hero meets the mentor who guides, gives gifts, and leads the heroes to the place of victory.

- The hero's journey is always the journey down and then up.
- It's a journey we engage despite our weakness.
- It's a journey that requires recognition of our antagonist, our enemy.
- It's a journey that leads us to embrace our mentor, our friend, our sage, our discipler—and in that relationship to receive fresh gifts and seeing new victory.
- Finally, it's a journey from which we emerge with bounties and blessings that we can share with others.

The reason the hero's journey is so ubiquitously found in the Bible and across the stories and mythologies of so many cultures is that this narrative frame is built into every facet of our lives—whether it's the cause we're passionate about, the fight to move beyond a traumatic event in our past, or even the everyday struggle of raising children. It is integrated into the expectations of every experience we have. Donald Miller argues that it doesn't really matter what experience you've had. Everybody's life story is a story of recognizing a sense of purpose and encountering difficulty in that, and then overcoming it.[5]

The hero's journey is the connecting idea between all the heroic stories we find in the Bible. As already mentioned, the warp and weft of the Bible is covenant and kingdom. These

---

5   Donald Miller, *A Million Miles in a Thousand Years* (Nashville, TN: Thomas Nelson, 2009).

two elements—one the King speaking about our call and fundamentally responsibility to represent him (Kingdom), and the same King extending his arms to all of us as our Father (Covenant)—are frozen for a moment on Mount Calvary. There, one Hero died as a substitute for all the lost, wayward children of God and as our champion defeating the enemies of death, sin, and Satan.[6]

As the Bible unfolds these two great themes, it reveals the connecting framework of the hero's journey. God sends his son as a hero revealed in the person of Jesus. We understand this journey as we can grasp the breadth of all that God does among his people, as he weaves together relationship and responsibility. As we do, we understand the story of Jesus, the archetypical hero, and we also understand our own call to take the same journey.

The hero's journey is the way that every great story in the Bible is told. Every great heroine and every great hero follows the same pattern, a common path, toward a divinely defined destiny. By understanding the pattern, we understand the path of the life of Jesus, and we understand the pattern and path of our own calling.

Think about Ruth and her heroic journey. Clearly, this is a journey down into a metaphysical valley and then up toward a gracious fulfillment. Clearly, it began with a call she embraced—the call to stay with her mother-in-law. Naomi also served as her mentor, as did Boaz, her "kinsman redeemer," first from afar and then growing as a husband. And clearly, Ruth received bounties and blessings at the completion of her journey—the bounty and blessing of providing for Naomi and establishing this line of King David. From this lineage the Savior Jesus would ensue. This compact little narrative from the Old Testament is a clear example of the hero's journey that we find over and over in Scripture. We find it in the life of Joseph, David, Esther, and so many more.

---

6   You can see models and qualifiers at work as you consider the hero's journey and Covenant and Kingdom in parallel.

LOOKING AT OUR LIFE AS A HERO'S JOURNEY

As I look back, I can see that I've been on a hero's journey in the past couple of years. I've really engaged with the weaknesses that I know are within me—the besetting sins and the regular temptations. And I've come to a point of recognition, realization, and resolution about many of those. Some of those have come to me by way of accusation by others, but most of them have been addressed by the gentle and convicting work of the Holy Spirit ministering within me.

As I've approached the end of this journey, I've begun to realize that there's a new phase of the mission that God has given me. In the beginning of my life as a Christian, God called me to be a missionary, and very quickly called me to a preaching and teaching role within the local church. I became a Christian at the age of 16, and from the age of 18 I was in seminary, training in various ways both inside and outside of the academy. Sometimes I was on the frontline of inner-city communities doing face-to-face youth work, and the other times I was in the classroom doing graduate or postgraduate theology.

By the time I was 25, I was ordained into the Church of England, and I functioned for the next 10 years as a missionary to the under-resourced people and communities to which God had called our Family on Mission.

And then there was a moment when the Lord stepped in and appeared to say, "I'm going to take you into the 'desert.' Then I'm going to put it all together for you, and I'm going to show you what needs to unfold in your life and mission." Sally and I and our young family went off to Arkansas for a few years, returning to our mission in England as I was called to lead a church in Sheffield. What happened next was an amazing breakthrough led out through a preaching ministry on Sundays and a face-to-face discipling work for the rest of the week. This breakthrough cascaded out into more and more huddles and missional communities (we called them clusters in those days). Eventually what happened during those 10 years in Sheffield spawned a movement that has now touched hundreds of thousands of people worldwide.

My work naturally transitioned into the phase of movement leadership at the end of this season. As a movement leader, I invested in local church leaders in different part of the world. My family moved to the States to help develop that. The Lord seemed to be telling us to do this so that we could work with a broader canvas and wider platform from a U.S. base. Sure enough, we were able to lead the movement as it spread in Europe out across the States and the other continents of the world.

And then we saw that journey draw to a close. There was a moment a few years ago when the Lord seemed to clearly say, "I want you to decentralize 3DM (the movement I led). I want you to hand over the leadership of the Order of Mission (one of the expressions of the movement especially in Europe). I want you to step out of public roles of ministry—just like you did in your early 30s. I want you to go into the 'desert,' and I'm going to put it all together, and we'll see a new phase begin to unfold." The last few years have been a journey into academic study and coaching leaders in unlocking the content you're discovering in this book, and now it is has led me back to the pulpit.. I am convinced that, just as with my last time in the desert, this period of pruning, retreat, rebound, and abiding in Christ will lead to significant breakthroughs in my families of mission.

When you look at these experiences through the model of the hero's journey, it's easy to see the pattern. It's a pattern that repeats itself throughout your life and mine. And that means that when you enter the "desert" or the "valley," whether for the first time or for one more of the many times you journeyed there, you can trust you will be given breakthroughs on the other side. Can you map your journey?

I hope you find this encouraging, because I know many of you go through these phases when you find yourself in the desert or in the valley. When we're in the desert, what we're called to do is dig wells. Sometimes we need to empty wells that have been dug earlier, as Isaac did with the wells of Abraham for instance. Sometimes we need to dig fresh wells. But the wells always lead us to the same water, the same source of life, the same creative reality that is the Lord himself pouring himself out to us and out from us to others.

So if you're in your desert, my encouragement to you is to keep digging.

Keep wrestling with the Lord.

Keep praying.

Keep reading the Scriptures.

Keep listening.

Keep reflecting.

Keep digging.

Excavate in the desert until you find the gold you can share with others.

It may be that you find in the desert that there's an antagonist who wants to expose your weaknesses and sins. But look for the mentor, the blessed Holy Spirit, working often through a human "discipling" agent, who will bring you gifts, bring you insights, bring you an understanding and comfort and encouragement to keep going.

And when you see the breakthrough and win the victory, the Lord will have you share the spoils of war, the blessings and the boons, with others. This is the heroic journey of faith of 2 Timothy: "For I am already being poured out like a drink offering, and the time for my departure is near. I have fought the good fight, I have finished the race, I have kept the faith."[7]

We will unpack the hero's journey in much more detail in the next few chapters. But for now, it's enough to recognize that we are all hardwired with this journey in our culture and in our

---

7   2 Timothy 4:6-7

lives. This will help you start to recognize the hero's journey in your past, your present, and your future.

BROKEN HEROES, ONE AND ALL

As we talk about the hero's journey, it's important that you don't think of a paragon of virtue like Superman or Captain America. Real heroes have checkered pasts and troubled histories, yet they can still become heroically fruitful.

The American culture has started to get it. There's a reason that every hero you see stories about today—from Iron Man to Princess Elsa—has an internal vulnerability.

Campbell argues that broken heroes are the heroes we actually resonate with most. He contends that we like our heroes broken because we want them to be like us.

This is wonderful news for us, because we ourselves can only be heroes of the broken variety. We may find it difficult to admit it in public, but in our hearts we all know we are imperfect, and we fear that these internal inadequacies disqualify us from achieving greatness. We want to see heroic stories lived by people who overcome their internal struggles, giving us hope that we too might do something great.

The problem is that all of us struggle with the challenges of life. However capable we are, we wrestle with internal issues that cause us to harbor nagging fears that we're not quite up to the mark. And so we choose heroes who reveal that it's possible to do great things, even with failings. In fact, it might be fair to say that we don't just want our heroes this way—we need them this way. As we identify with broken heroes, we grasp answers to deep questions that would remain unanswered without these flawed examples.

But our world leads us to try to hide our brokenness, instead of embracing it. We live in an affirmation culture increasingly defined by achievement. In our culture, inadequacy often leads to the removal of affirmation. The removal of affirmation by those around us has a much older moniker in human history. It's called shame.

Shame besets the lives of so many of us. We feel shame about our family, shame about our education, shame about our past, shame about our weight, shame about our income, and shame about the things we've done and things we've found it impossible to do. We feel shame very deeply and want someone to lift it away. That's why the heroes we choose are so important. The broken hero overcomes his or her greatest challenge by winning through the internal struggles that so often lead to rejection by others. Victory is found on the other side of shame.

Just like broken heroes, we need to overcome the shadow of shame to grasp the torch of victory.

The marvel of the gospel we embrace and proclaim is that you and I are not under the curse of shame. We are under a grace that replaces every shame with a blessing.

Jesus is our all in all. He not only paid the penalty of our failures and sins, but he also buried the shame that was attached to them. We don't have to hide our failures anymore because they are not attached to shame; they are simply examples of what God can do with failures like us.

We often say in the movement of missional discipleship that people don't need a perfect example—they just need a living example. That actually means we don't need perfect examples—we need broken examples that reveal that the shame of inadequacy can be overcome by the blessings of grace.

That's why it's so important for you and I to recognize two things; first, that we are inadequate to the heroic task of making disciples; and second, we need not carry any shame in the fact that we are broken heroes.

We are inadequate because everyone is, and no one in and of himself or herself has the capacity or the ability to make a single disciple. Only by God's all-encompassing grace are we able to fulfill such a high and heroic calling. Others need someone just like you and me—they need broken heroes.

You may be asking, "But about what about Jesus? He wasn't broken, was he?" Consider this.

- He was a failure in the eyes of religious leaders
- On the Cross, he was "cursed."
- His followers regularly messed up.
- He did not have many friends in "high places."
- Rome considered him insignificant and of no importance.

So maybe Jesus was not a failure in our eyes, but in everyone else's eyes he was. Perhaps this was Judas' major stumbling block.

COMMUNICATING THE HERO'S JOURNEY

By now you have a grasp on what the hero's journey is, and how it resonates with just about everyone because it is so pervasive. But how do we communicate biblically and awaken the people we speak to a deeper experience of a genuine God-given reality?

First, we must connect the hero's journey to our personal gospel. Consider how we can understand the life of Jesus via the pattern of the hero's journey.

- He embraces his calling.
- He enters the desert to face his enemy.
- He takes on the challenge and sickness and spiritual oppression, and with the help of his Father ("I only do what I see my Father doing"[8]).
- He gathers friends and allies who commit themselves to his quest.
- He fulfills his great quest to save the world.

---

8   John 5:19

- He brings about victory so he can share the spoils of victory.

The Apostle Paul described Jesus' heroic journey this way:

In your relationships with one another, have the same mindset as Christ Jesus:

Who, being in very nature God,
did not consider equality with God something to be
used to his own advantage;
rather, he made himself nothing
by taking the very nature of a servant,
being made in human likeness.
And being found in appearance as a man,
he humbled himself
by becoming obedient to death—
even death on a cross!

Therefore God exalted him to the highest place
and gave him the name that is above every name,
that at the name of Jesus every knee should bow,
in heaven and on earth and under the earth,
and every tongue acknowledge that Jesus Christ is Lord,
to the glory of God the Father.[9]

Jesus' recapitulation of human life shows us that the objective of every person is to take on the task of the hero's journey. We are to take up our cross and follow him (our calling), go through this world that is not our home, and embrace the challenge of bringing an awakening of discipleship in the lives of others with the help of the Father, Son, and Holy Spirit. One day, we will enjoy the spoils of victory with Jesus. But along the way, the small victories will reveal that we will share the fruit and gifts of the Spirit with the people around us along the way.

---

9   Philippians 2:5-11

By explaining our gospel through the model of the hero's journey, we help other people understand our gospel and see how it relates to the metanarrative of Scripture.

We can of course connect our journey to the heroic stories of Scripture, and also to the context and culture in which we live. These bridges of resonance become natural entry points into the lives of people who need good news, and they enable us to connect to the individuals to whom we speak. People already have a picture of the way they want their life to go, and it's thoroughly consistent with a Biblical worldview on the hero's journey.

If you know that, you'll be able to do something that very few people are able to do—you'll be able to speak directly to the culture, because you have listened to what it is that is the fabric of this culture. You'll get a sense of the important elements of your culture, and, because you know the components of the communicative frame, you'll be able to speak with real effectiveness.

That opens up the hugely exciting process of conversion and awakening. How does that happen? It happens as people become aware of what God is calling them to do. It happens even as these broken heroes acknowledge the real challenges they face on their journeys. And ultimately, it reaches completion as the heroes faithfully follow Jesus until they experience the kind of spiritual awakening that only God can bring.

CALL

COMPLETION

CHALLENGE

In summary:

- The hero becomes aware of the call God has placed on his or her life
- The hero acknowledges the challenge the call presents and the need it addresses
- The hero is awakened into a life of discipleship and mission

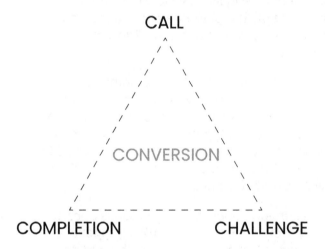

CALL

CONVERSION

COMPLETION   CHALLENGE

Using the hero's journey will help us make the way from content to context to conversion.

Let's look at how this works in more detail.

TEN

THE CALL

Aware of my Call
The Cost of the Call
Particular Calls
The Call Starts the Journey

As I've already mentioned, I'm a bit of a cinephile. So when I think of the hero's journey, my mind naturally goes to the heroes I have seen on screen.

For any of these heroes, there is a moment where they are awakened and become aware of an overriding call for the first time. In this moment, their eyes are opened, they become compassionate, and they must make a choice of whether to respond to this new awareness, or try to ignore it and move on with their lives.

The movies that really nail this become iconic. Think of these moments:

- Thomas Anderson becomes aware of the matrix, and faces the choice of whether to become Neo and fight against it. This is so memorable that many of us use the idea of taking the red pill or the blue pill as a metaphor for the turning points of our lives.
- Erin Brockovich learns that a gas and electric company has contaminated the water in Hinkley, California, and

goes on a crusade to sue the company and get justice for the hundreds of people affected.

- Jim Kirk realizes he can be like his father and become a Starfleet captain
- T'Challa, mourning the loss of his father, realizes he can be a great King of Wakanda like his father, and he embraces his role and responsibility as Black Panther.
- The list goes on and on…

You get the idea. The inciting event that evokes a call could uncover some injustice or evil, or unveil an opportunity for greatness. The hero becomes aware of the call, and feels led to respond by starting on the hero's journey.

This awareness can even come in a still, small voice. If I whispered the phrase "If you build it, he will come," your mind would go to the baseball field that Ray Kinsella builds in *Field of Dreams*. These supernatural voices take Ray on a hero's journey that result in him getting to play baseball with his father one last time—and save the family farm in the process.

This kind of supernatural awareness doesn't just happen in cornfields in Iowa. We find a remarkably similar story at the start of Samuel's heroic journey.

> *The boy Samuel ministered before the Lord under Eli. In those days the word of the Lord was rare; there were not many visions.*
>
> *One night Eli, whose eyes were becoming so weak that he could barely see, was lying down in his usual place. The lamp of God had not yet gone out, and Samuel was lying down in the house of the Lord, where the ark of God was. Then the Lord called Samuel.*
>
> *Samuel answered, "Here I am." And he ran to Eli and said, "Here I am; you called me."*
>
> *But Eli said, "I did not call; go back and lie down." So he went and lay down.*

Again the Lord called, "Samuel!" And Samuel got up and went to Eli and said, "Here I am; you called me."

"My son," Eli said, "I did not call; go back and lie down."

Now Samuel did not yet know the Lord: The word of the Lord had not yet been revealed to him.

A third time the Lord called, "Samuel!" And Samuel got up and went to Eli and said, "Here I am; you called me."

Then Eli realized that the Lord was calling the boy. So Eli told Samuel, "Go and lie down, and if he calls you, say, 'Speak, Lord, for your servant is listening.'" So Samuel went and lay down in his place.

The Lord came and stood there, calling as at the other times, "Samuel! Samuel!"

Then Samuel said, "Speak, for your servant is listening."

And the Lord said to Samuel: "See, I am about to do something in Israel that will make the ears of everyone who hears about it tingle."[1]

From this point, Samuel started even as a young boy prophesying what God was going to do—first to Eli, and before long to all of Israel. He was aware of his call, and ready to embark on his hero's journey. And of course it was built on the equally impressive heroic story of Hannah his mother.

If we are going to go on the hero's journey, we need to ask ourselves what our mission as heroes really is. What is our mission as we seek to imitate and emulate the life of Jesus, who is our Lord? Since he is the one who we follow, what then is the path that we follow on this hero's journey?

A story of a hero's journey from the Bible will help us tremendously. Let's turn to the life of Paul, one of the great heroes of the New Testament. Near the end of his story, when he is standing before King Agrippa, Paul describes the call of

---

1   1 Samuel 3:1-11

his journey as a hero. Paul has been arrested in Jerusalem and has been spirited away by the Roman governor and guards, to Caesarea, which is a great Roman compound. And there he has met with, both the former and the current governor of the people and has told his story before these great governors and kings. In the middle of this exchange, he speaks about the start of his own journey to Jesus, and his own journey, that began with him being a persecutor of the people of God.

"I too was convinced that I ought to do all that was possible to oppose the name of Jesus of Nazareth. And that is just what I did in Jerusalem. On the authority of the chief priests I put many of the Lord's people in prison, and when they were put to death, I cast my vote against them. Many a time I went from one synagogue to another to have them punished, and I tried to force them to blaspheme. I was so obsessed with persecuting them that I even hunted them down in foreign cities.

"On one of these journeys I was going to Damascus with the authority and commission of the chief priests. About noon, King Agrippa, as I was on the road, I saw a light from heaven, brighter than the sun, blazing around me and my companions. We all fell to the ground, and I heard a voice saying to me in Aramaic, 'Saul, Saul, why do you persecute me? It is hard for you to kick against the goads.'

"Then I asked, 'Who are you, Lord?'

" 'I am Jesus, whom you are persecuting,' the Lord replied. 'Now get up and stand on your feet. I have appeared to you to appoint you as a servant and as a witness of what you have seen and will see of me. I will rescue you from your own people and from the Gentiles. I am sending you to them to open their eyes and turn them from darkness to light, and from the power of Satan to God, so that they may receive forgiveness of

*sins and a place among those who are sanctified by faith
in me.'*

*"So then, King Agrippa, I was not disobedient to the
vision from heaven. First to those in Damascus, then
to those in Jerusalem and in all Judea, and then to the
Gentiles, I preached that they should repent and turn to
God and demonstrate their repentance by their deeds."* [2]

We don't often focus on this particular version of Paul's
conversion. We read the one in Acts 9 which is part of the
narrative that Luke unfolds. But here, from the words of Paul
himself, we discover details that had not previously been
articulated. We have the words that Jesus spoke directly to
Paul (then Saul) about what Jesus saw in his life. And we also
see the bigger and broader commission and calling that Jesus
gave Paul as he sent him on mission, not as a willing witness,
but as one who was plucked out of his ordinary life, and set on
a course that would change him forever, and change the world
forever.

Paul is called and sent on a mission, and there is no
discussion as to whether he's going to say yes or no. Isn't that
interesting?

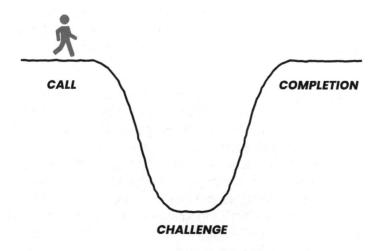

CALL

COMPLETION

CHALLENGE

AWARE OF MY CALL

I've never been called to build a baseball field in Iowa, or to choose between a red pill or blue pill. But throughout my life I have become aware of the call for new seasons of ministry.

As I've already shown in this book, my life can be traced as a rhythmic pattern of being pruned in preparation for a new season of ministry, and then fruitfulness within that ministry. These rhythms have roughly occurred every decade since I first entered ministry back in the 1980s.

Early on, I ministered in the inner city area of Brixton. While there was certainly fruit during this time, both personally and in my ministry, at the end of that season Sally and I were completely worn out. We needed to step back for a time to figure out how to better minister in a healthy rhythm for our family.

In that way, we were kind of like Indiana Jones realizing that his relationship with his father was more important than even the most hallowed archeological discovery—the Holy Grail— in 1989's *Indiana Jones and the Last Crusade*. We had to recalibrate how to do Family on Mission.

After a time of pruning in Arkansas, I returned to England to minister in Sheffield. This was a time of incredible fruit, marked by a newfound understanding of how discipleship was the catalyst that mobilized and, more importantly, sustained mission.

This journey was almost like what Simba experiences in 1994's *The Lion King*, as he learned from mentors like Zazu the bird and later from Timon and Pumbaa. This was essential for Simba before he becomes king, because of the gap created in his life by the loss of his father. This film resonated in the 1990s because so many people had seen their nuclear families fall apart. Vehicles like missional communities that provided a place for Family on Mission to thrive were so vital during this time in awakening people in Sheffield (and far beyond) to the call Jesus was giving them.

After my time in Sheffield, my family moved again to the States, first to Arizona and then to Pawleys Island, South Carolina. This happened because God awakened me to the call to be a movemental leader. How could I train churches and leaders around the world in the kind of discipleship that had impacted so many in Sheffield?

In many ways, this call reflected what we saw on screen with Frodo Baggins in *The Lord of the Rings* trilogy, or with Harry Potter in a series of eight movies through the decade. Both received the call to take on epic quests that would change their worlds, and they had to figure out how to do that.

After several years, God awakened me to the call of decentralizing 3DM. It was time for another time of pruning, and a time for me to analyze the communication style I had been doing intuitively and understand why it worked and how it could be usefully imitated by others for the advancement of the Kingdom of God. This book is the fruit of this time.

The journey is a bit like 2010's *Inception*, in which hero Dom Cobb receives a call to take his expertise and express it in an entirely new way—by putting an idea into someone's head via dream, instead of simply stealing information away through dreams.

The call starts the hero's journey, and as you can see from my example, it also happens many times during a hero's journey. It's almost as if the journey is laps of a race, or perhaps stages of a triathlon. At times, God calls us to pivot our approach through a new call.

A Scriptural example of this kind of pivot comes when God awakens Peter to the call to minister to Gentiles, not just Jews.

> *About noon the following day as they were on their journey and approaching the city, Peter went up on the roof to pray. He became hungry and wanted something to eat, and while the meal was being prepared, he fell into a trance. He saw heaven opened and something like a large sheet being let down to earth by its four*

*corners. It contained all kinds of four-footed animals, as
well as reptiles and birds. Then a voice told him, "Get up,
Peter. Kill and eat."*

*"Surely not, Lord!" Peter replied. "I have never eaten
anything impure or unclean."*

*The voice spoke to him a second time, "Do not call
anything impure that God has made clean."*

*This happened three times, and immediately the sheet
was taken back to heaven.*[3]

We should expect God to call us to the hero's journey time and
time again. And as communicators, we should seek to awaken
those we disciple and speak to time and time again. Obviously,
we can focus on how to do this in a way that awakens people
to salvation, but the call to mission and discipleship will re-
emerge time and again if we are open to it.

THE COST OF THE CALL

One thing that is difficult for people to understand is that
embracing the call God gives you almost always means
giving up what you have. That's the only way to go on a hero's
journey.

No wonder so many stories tell us about reluctant heroes, who
initially don't want to accept the call they have been given.
There is conflict in the inciting incident, and the hero must
wrestle with the idea of sacrifice before embracing the call.
Bruce Wayne must choose between being a hero or having a
future with Rachel Dawes, the love of his life. He chooses to
be a hero, and Batman is born.

Obviously, the greatest example of this is the cost Jesus paid
to embrace his call to rescue the world. No wonder the devil

---

3   Acts 10:9-16

tempted him with glory and riches at the beginning of his ministry—Jesus had given up so much.[4]

Following the hero's journey means following Jesus' example of sacrifice. There is no other way. Your call will inevitably include a challenge. (More on this in the next chapter.)

Now that's not something we want to hear. After all, we have quite a high opinion of our individual importance and significance. Perhaps that's rightly so, because if there were only one of us, Jesus would have come just for us. And if there were only one waiting on his return, he would return for us. It doesn't matter which way you look at it—you can't say that the individual is not important.

But somehow we have extrapolated this truth into a belief that we're more important than God, more important than his plan for us, and that we're somehow more significant than the call that he places upon us.

The only thing God wants us to do is to fulfill our destiny as his child, and this requires that we come to a place where we know what it means, not only to fulfill something, but also to be personally fulfilled ourselves. God has designed us for things that are generally true of all other people, and he has also designed you for a journey, a particular path, a particular mission. He is shaping you right now so that you can fulfill it.

No matter where you go in the Bible, you find God choosing people, sometimes from the upper echelons of society (Moses[5]) and sometimes from the lowest echelon of society (the woman at the well[6]). You find God choosing men and women. Look in the Bible, and you find that, whoever you are, male or female, young or old, on the margins of society or at the centers of power, God has a call for you and has a place for you.

---

4   See Philippians 2:5-11 and 2 Corinthians 8:9.

5   Cf. Exodus 3.

6   Cf John 4.

A side note here: Our equality is found in a couple of really important things. Our equality is based on the fact that God's grace is equally provided to every person on this planet, without conditions. You can't have a greater expression of equality than that. There is no distinction. There is no variation in the way that God approaches each person on the planet, He gives us all the same apportionment of grace for salvation. But here's the thing: beyond that absolute equality, there is another equality that God wants you to embrace. He calls every single one of us to be his representative. It doesn't matter whether your representation is to the homeless person, the hungry person, the marginalized person, or to the corridors of power.

And as you embrace that calling and that mission, as James puts it, if you're rich, then you're glad to become poor. And if you're poor, then you're overjoyed to know that you share in the king's wealth.[7] The call costs you everything and gives you everything.

PARTICULAR CALLS

In every case, the hero's journey begins with an incident, usually one designed by God. Sometimes, it is an (apparently) accidental occasion into which God enters. Sometimes, it is direct or even miraculous. Whichever way it occurs, something arrests your attention and calls you to think about life differently.

Paul was definitely arrested like this on the road to Damascus by the bright light shining and flashing around him and by the voice from heaven. His companions fell to the ground, and so does he. From this point forward, his life is never going to be the same again. He's on the ground, groveling in the dust, and Jesus reveals to him two amazing things: his destiny and the people of whom he's now going to be part.

Like Paul, Peter has one of the great conversions of the New Testament. At both of these conversions, Jesus reveals at their conversion not only their destiny but also their gospel and the

7   James 1:9-11

context to which they will minister throughout their lives. For Peter, the call is to build the church (literally the called-out ones). For Paul, the call is about the body of Christ. I don't know if you've ever considered that, but at the moment Paul met Jesus on the road to Damascus, the revelation of the "Body of Christ" began. How do I know? Because Jesus says, "Why do you persecute me?" Paul asks, "Who are you, Lord" The answer is, "I am Jesus, whom you are persecuting."

Paul spent the next three years in the desert, and probably 10 total years in obscurity. Think of all those occasions and opportunities he had to reflect on the words of Jesus. *When I hurt a Christian, Jesus felt it. How can it be that, when I locked up a man and separated him from his family, Jesus experienced that? How can it be that when that woman was whipped in front of the synagogue, Jesus felt it? How can it be that, when we cast our lot against that criminal element within the synagogue, and we killed them, Jesus experienced it? What is that?*

We see later how Paul came to understand this: I'm sure he came to the realization that, "It's almost like they're so connected to him that you'd have to say that the people of Jesus are his 'body.'" You can see where that revelation came from. It happened right there at the beginning, as he chose to step across the threshold from a life of Phariseeism and strict religious observance into a life pursuing the call of Jesus. At that moment so much revelation was dropped into his heart.

You may feel that you don't really know that much right now, but I can absolutely assure you that everything that you will ever need to know has already been imparted to you by revelation at your salvation. Now, it may well take the rest of your life for you to understand and express that revelation, but everything that you've ever needed to know has been imparted to your spirit already. Otherwise, it's not worth being a Christian. You may as well join another religion that requires years of training and learning and education. The Bible and faith in Jesus tells us that he comes and takes up residence. Do you need any more revelation than that? If God himself comes and lives within us, how much more do we need?

When Jesus came and took up residence in Paul, Paul didn't need anything else from that point on. He just had to become familiar with what Jesus had come to do. He had to learn what it was. He had to understand it. He had to embrace it. In other words, he had to go on the journey. But that moment of revelation came in a way particular to Paul. It was different to Peter. It was different to Stephen. It was different to Mary and Elizabeth. But in every case, it was still Jesus. And it was consistent with all of the heroic journeys of God's faithful people in Scriptures.

Before we move on, reflect on this question: Where are you in this journey of understanding the particular call that is yours and yours alone?

The revelation that you needed has already taken place. God comes in and takes up residence in your life. He doesn't creep in over your lifetime. He doesn't insinuate himself into your life. He doesn't operate like a bad smell. He comes and takes up residence, and in taking up residence he brings with him all of the necessary revelation that will save you, that will sanctify you, and that will send you on the journey and the adventure of a lifetime.

THE CALL STARTS THE JOURNEY

Let's focus again on how Paul described his conversion in front of Agrippa and Festus. It's important that we look at how Paul describes it, because we often fall into the mindset that we want our journeys to be more developed than they already are. We want to join the journey not at the beginning, but sort of halfway through.

But God calls us to start at square one. He knows better than us how to unfold a mission, and he knows better than us what it means to begin the process of embracing a journey that will last a lifetime.

I use a picture (you and I both know now that it's a meme) to explain the beginning of a journey. There are two mountainsides, and between them is a valley. The journey of faith always embraces a valley. Sometimes the Bible uses other metaphors—the desert, or the far side of the mountain. The journey starts with a call that comes by God's choice.

In Paul's case, God didn't knock quietly—he came in like a hurricane. God calls Paul to be his servant and to be his witness to a particular people group.

Eventually Paul gets there. We know this people group is the Gentiles, because whenever Paul writes the letters of the New Testament, at the beginning he says "Paul, an apostle to the Gentiles."[8] He knows to whom he has been sent. And he knows that this call will inevitably involve enormous challenge, not the least of which is death at the hands of the Jewish authorities. But as he says in Philippians, he has heard the heavenward call and has decided to take hold of that for which Christ Jesus has taken hold of him.

Because there is a challenge, and one that takes place in the valley, we need to be clear about the call from the start of the journey. It begs the question: To whom are you called? The truth will come out under pressure at some point, but it's best to know at the start of the journey. Paul did, as we see later in his address to Agrippa.

> So then, King Agrippa, I was not disobedient to the vision from heaven. First to those in Damascus, then to those in Jerusalem and in all Judea, and then to the Gentiles, I preached that they should repent and turn to God and demonstrate their repentance by their deeds.[9]

Where are you supposed to start? Paul was supposed to start in Damascus—right where he was. When he finished in Damascus and couldn't do any more there, then he was to go to Jerusalem. From there to Judea, and on from there. It sounds a lot like what Jesus told the disciples before he ascended—when the Holy Spirit comes upon you, you will be

---

8   Philippians 3:12-14

9   Acts 26:19-20

my witnesses. First, right here. Next, just over there. Next, a little bit further over there. And then, when you've done all that, you can go everywhere else. We saw Jesus tell this to the disciples, and here we see it translated to Paul's context.

I became a Christian at 16, and the Lord called me to be a missionary. As a missionary, you start with your family. You start with your neighbors. You start with your workmates. You start with your colleagues at school or at college. You start where you are, and then you'll get to where God wants to lead you. For me, he has led me from my family hometown in England—I was privileged to see my parents come to Christ—to other places like Brixton and Sheffield, and then across the pond to America, where I now live, and to many other places all over the world.

It's the same pattern we find in Jesus. Jesus entered the wilderness full of the Holy Spirit, and came out of the wilderness full of the *power* of the Holy Spirit.[10] Then where did he go? He went home to Nazareth. Why didn't he go to Jerusalem straight away? Why didn't he go to the people at the top of the religious heap? Because he was giving us the pattern of our heroic journey. He was giving us the picture of what it was all of his followers are expected to do. Jesus would tell the disciples they should start in Jerusalem and then go to Judea, Samaria, and the ends of the world. But I think that's because they were to start where they were. Jesus started where he was raised in Nazareth and Galilee. This kind of adventure gets to be real fun, but let's start where we're called to start.

Once we've started the hero's journey, we come to the point where we begin to acknowledge the *challenge*. As we enter into the difficulty of the journey, we will undoubtedly enter a valley or desert in our lives. We even run the risk of losing our call as heroes. That's what the next chapter is all about.

But before we get to the valley, it's imperative that we are clear about the *call* so we remember what the hero's journey is all

---

10   Luke 4:11-14

about. So let's renew our commitment to follow the call we are now aware of, and let's renew our commitment to start where Jesus wants us to start.

ELEVEN

THE CHALLENGE:
INTO THE VALLEY

The hero's journey begins with someone who is aware of the call. But it is rarely a straight line from there to the awakening that leads to fruitful breakthrough. As we follow the call of God, begin where we are, and follow the breadcrumbs of grace in ever-widening circles toward the frontiers of his mission, we will inevitably encounter challenges in the valley that will test the call.

We are enamored with the beginning and the end of the hero's journey. Traditionally, the church has focused on the call through evangelism and the completion through eschatology (the end times). But the challenge often has not had the same affection. Yet it is here that the source and process of discipleship is embraced,.

We love the story of the call, and we love the victory at the end. But the challenge in the middle of the story—the journey into the valley—is really the meat of the story. This is where we gain the things that actually make us heroes and help us enjoy the bountiful blessings that come at the end.

But we tend to get this backward. Think about how most Christians respond when a church pastor falls because of bad choices made morally or financially or in some other area. Christians don't usually see this person as a broken hero who will go through the valley; they simply see a failure and write that person off. Can you imagine what that must be like? Can you imagine if others treated you this way? This kind of reaction shows our desire to focus on only the high points of the hero's journey, and avoiding the more essential place of the valley.

The valley is where we face the biggest challenge of our journey. And so it is no surprise that we don't make it through the valley on our own. We need help and gifts from our mentor to make it through. We also need to learn skills and develop tools that will help us achieve the heroic outcome of our journey. We need these things because the challenge we face is huge. If it weren't massive, it wouldn't require a hero to overcome it.

To navigate the challenge through the valley, each of us needs to have something that is constantly calling us on, constantly guiding us from within, constantly speaking to us of the future, constantly counseling us about the steps that we should be taking. The Holy Spirit is the presence within us, the mentor

CALL

COMPLETION

CHALLENGE

on the journey. Once the people of God had presence without; now he is the presence within.

As we discussed in the first section of this book, the Holy Spirit will help you to craft your gospel. And when you apply the good news to yourself and make it your gospel, you now have a tool, a gift, a skill, an equipping that is designed by God for you and your journey—including the challenges. Your challenge is going to be different than my challenge, and that's why your expression of the gospel is particular to you and different than mine.

THE ENEMY AND THE VALLEY

The challenge in the valley is so large because it is there that we will face the enemy. Sometimes, this enemy is external. Obviously, this brings to mind Jesus facing the temptations of Satan before beginning his ministry. But sometimes, as with the scandal-ridden megachurch pastors we just mentioned, the enemy is also within.

All of us find an enemy in ourselves to some degree. This part of our personal makeup is in conflict with the journey we are going on. We might call it the flesh or our old selves or just plain rebellion; whatever the name, it is a very real issue in our lives. In his letter to the Colossians, Paul expressed how peace is a key to defeating the enemy within.

> Let the peace of Christ rule in your hearts, since as members of one body you were called to peace. And be thankful. Let the message of Christ dwell among you richly as you teach and admonish one another with all wisdom through psalms, hymns, and songs from the Spirit, singing to God with gratitude in your hearts. And whatever you do, whether in word or deed, do it all in the name of the Lord Jesus, giving thanks to God the Father through him.[1]

---

1   Colossians 3:15-17

Paul says that peace in our hearts is a gift, and we should let it be the referee[2] in our hearts. Peace is something we discover as a gift from Jesus, and it functions as a referee, blowing the whistle to stop the action and correct our behavior when our external or internal peace is violated by the enemy within.

The way the hero can overcome the enemy within by engaging the voice of the mentor on the daily basis. Is peace present in you? Is it ruling? Are you thankful? Thankfulness is almost a litmus test for peace in our lives. Then, as we are ruled by peace, we will grow in the word and in community with each other, and we will be able to do everything in the name of Jesus and not out of bondage to the enemy within.

WHAT THE VALLEY REVEALS

Let's return to Paul's story again, to see how his gospel emerged as a gift from God on his journey. Before we read this passage, it's important to remember that Paul was writing to a specific situation in the church in Corinth, where leaders were seeking to demean Paul and suggest that his message to the church was of little significance.

> Are they Hebrews? So am I. Are they Israelites? So am I. Are they Abraham's descendants? So am I. Are they servants of Christ? (I am out of my mind to talk like this.) I am more. I have worked much harder, been in prison more frequently, been flogged more severely, and been exposed to death again and again. Five times I received from the Jews the forty lashes minus one. Three times I was beaten with rods, once I was pelted with stones, three times I was shipwrecked, I spent a night and a day in the open sea, I have been constantly on the move. I have been in danger from rivers, in danger from bandits, in danger from my fellow Jews, in danger from Gentiles; in danger in the city, in danger in the country,

---

2   The word translated rule in verse 15 is unique in the New Testament, and is best translated as *arbitrator* or *referee*.

*in danger at sea; and in danger from false believers. I
have labored and toiled and have often gone without
sleep; I have known hunger and thirst and have often
gone without food; I have been cold and naked. Besides
everything else, I face daily the pressure of my concern
for all the churches. Who is weak, and I do not feel
weak? Who is led into sin, and I do not inwardly burn?*

*If I must boast, I will boast of the things that show my
weakness. The God and Father of the Lord Jesus, who
is to be praised forever, knows that I am not lying. In
Damascus the governor under King Aretas had the city
of the Damascenes guarded in order to arrest me. But I
was lowered in a basket from a window in the wall and
slipped through his hands.*

*I must go on boasting. Although there is nothing to be
gained, I will go on to visions and revelations from the
Lord. I know a man in Christ who fourteen years ago
was caught up to the third heaven. Whether it was in the
body or out of the body I do not know—God knows. And
I know that this man—whether in the body or apart from
the body I do not know, but God knows—was caught
up to paradise and heard inexpressible things, things
that no one is permitted to tell. I will boast about a man
like that, but I will not boast about myself, except about
my weaknesses. Even if I should choose to boast, I
would not be a fool, because I would be speaking the
truth. But I refrain, so no one will think more of me than
is warranted by what I do or say, or because of these
surpassingly great revelations. Therefore, in order to
keep me from becoming conceited, I was given a thorn
in my flesh, a messenger of Satan, to torment me. Three
times I pleaded with the Lord to take it away from
me. But he said to me, "My grace is sufficient for you, for
my power is made perfect in weakness." Therefore I will
boast all the more gladly about my weaknesses, so that
Christ's power may rest on me. That is why, for Christ's
sake, I delight in weaknesses, in insults, in hardships, in*

persecutions, in difficulties. For when I am weak, then I am strong.[3]

Paul was in the midst of a challenge to his leadership, to his apostleship, and to his role in the life of a church he had planted with blood and sweat and tears. In the midst of that time, he was drawn again to the elements of his gospel. It was his gospel, personal to him and powerful to eloquently speak to him and to the lives of others.

When you look at Paul's life, you find elements in the landscape of his life that are similar to the elements in your life and mine. He had the eruptive moments. He had the erosive moments. He had the earthquake events, and he had excavations when he was able him to be able to dig into what it was that God had for him. Below the surface of his

---

3   2 Corinthians 11:22-12:10

life, the presence of God was like a volcano that erupted to the surface, when he was carried into the third heaven. But also, the presence of God below the surface of his life was exposed by the erosive forces of difficulty, of pain, of trial, of persecution.[4]

The presence of God came to the surface through the fault lines in his personality that were exposed in the earthquake-like upheavals in his life. Those earthquakes shook him when he was shipwrecked. He was in the open sea for a day and a night. He was in danger from bandits pursuing him. These shocking experiences exposed the fault lines in his personality, and as they were revealed, something came through the brokenness, the fear, the anxiety, and the stress. It was God's presence, which would have been hidden within had it not been for the earthquake showing where the fault line was. The

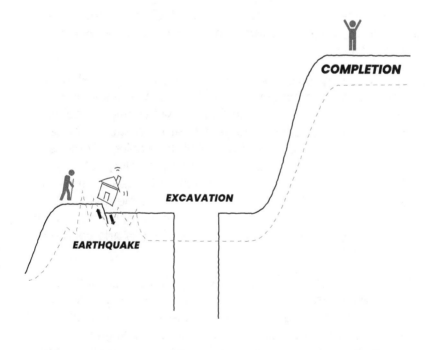

COMPLETION

EXCAVATION

EARTHQUAKE

---

4   Compare this with the first section of this book as we talked about the "Landscape of Life."

hidden presence of God would have remained hidden if not for the stripping of his life through the abrasive forces of difficulty.

Paul knew the eruptive presence of God, as we do. I hope that you like me are a Christian who is blessed to have regular experiences of God's eruptive presence. It's a wonderful thing. But there are so many other experiences that expose God's presence.

What about the difficulties?

What about the trials?

What about those grinding experiences that strip you back, wear you down, and erode your life and take back to the surface of your life to reveal the essential element below the service?

Do you have the same experience as Paul that, in the midst of this erosion, there is a surprising discovery that Jesus is in the midst of difficulty too?

In fact, one way we can look at the valley is to say that the we go through the landscape of life in the valley. We should not expect a simple trip down and then up; we should expect to spend time in the valley experiencing erosion and earthquakes and doing excavation. The process of developing our message happens in the valley, because being in the valley actually cultivates a sense of our own clarity and purpose in terms of the gospel we will bring. So as we develop a meme to picture the valley, we can actually put the landscape of life down in the valley, to show how our gospel develops in this arid yet fertile environment.

I have found this to be true. I've known times of chronic illness. I've known times of continual opposition. For several years I was tagged in social media and on the internet as a cult leader. I was invited to leave churches even though I was there simply to serve. I had to hold the hands of pastors who lost their jobs, simply because they wanted to disciple their people. I had to carry the burden of the knowledge that many people believed I'd gone astray. And yet in the midst of that, I found Jesus. His presence was even more real.

As well as knowing and meeting God in the erosions, I've also met God in the earthquakes. What's an earthquake? Well, it's a time of shocking sudden upheaval. Someone dies, there's a terrible accident, or something is lost—a job, a hope, an aspiration.

Just a few years ago, we lost our grandson. It was terrible, it came as an awful shock. One moment the whole family anticipates the birth of a baby boy, and the next moment there's an emergency caesarean, there are all kinds of medical emergencies and a week lived in a ward with our eldest daughter, and there is a little boy who didn't make it. All the brokenness inside of me was revealed. All the fault lines in my personality were exposed—all my tendencies toward anger and rage and sinfulness and revenge. Yet through those fault lines, God's presence was exposed. It may be that you have not had this kind of earthquake yet. But, without causing you to be afraid, I can assure you they'll come.

Paul knew all about the eruptions and the erosions and the earthquakes, so do you, and so do I.

We have many very personal ways to bear witness to the gospel. Paul's message was a message of grace—a message that the gift of Jesus the Messiah was a gift to the ancient people of God and to the people who never knew God. The grace of God is a gift of God seen in Jesus, a gift of relationship with God made possible by the death and resurrection of Jesus. This gift was not made simply to his ancient people, the Jews, but to all people. Paul's call was to take that message to Gentiles, people who had never known God, the Gentiles.

His emphasis of grace is of course applicable to everyone, but it was a particular message to a particular people group. His mission defined the message of his life. If you read Peter's letters, the book of James, and even the gospels, you can find the message of grace in there of course, but it's not central emphasis as it was for Paul.

So what is the emphasis in your witness to the gospel? If you ask my wife Sally, she will say God's faithfulness. And you know what? She's had an amazing ministry of sharing a gospel of faithfulness. It's amazing how many people need to hear that message. She shares this message directly and indirectly all the time.

If you ask me, I'll wriggle a little bit, but in the end I'll tell you my emphasis is that God lives within all believers and he speaks to us. The characteristic of God that I always come back to is that he lives within me and speaks to me. And you know what? It's amazing how many people need to know that God is not far off, that God is not above the heavens but closer to you than a brother, that he lives within you if you bow the knee to Jesus, and that he speaks to you face to face. It's an amazing thing.

I usually emphasize my message of good news this way, and it's been expressed by talking about how discipleship is really about answering two questions: What's God saying to you, and what are going to do about it? And you know what? Hundreds of thousands of people all over the world now ask those two questions most days of the week. It's the oddest thing that a working-class boy with dyslexia, for whom the Bible is the very first book he ever read, discovered that God wanted to speak to him, and that somehow this was a message he could carry to the world.

From my perspective on the gospel, I can see the whole gospel. I can't hear God unless he lives within me. And God cannot live within me unless he makes a relationship possible with me. And so I need the saving work of Jesus and I need the infilling work of the spirit.

You need to know what your witness to the gospel is. And then you need to hold onto it in the Valley of Elah, because holding onto it means holding onto God. David had a gospel—God is bigger than the lion and the bear and the battle belongs to the

Lord. David was able to pick up that word and sling it at a giant and bring him down.

I can't tell you the number of times that I've carried the knowledge of my gospel in my hand and wondered how it was going to help. Yet it always does in the challenges of the valley.

God is shaping you to carry a message. He's shaping you with the circumstances of your life, even in the valley, and causing his revelation of himself to be revealed in you. This revelation shows you this gospel and reveals Jesus to you. My encouragement to you is to go after that. Go after it. Carry your witness to the gospel, and as you carry that gospel, allow it to be the transforming reality in your life and in the lives of those that God puts in your way.

The people who know the message that God has given them are people who are powerful in the hands of God, because the challenges of life don't shake them. So little discourages them. They acknowledge the challenges, but these challenges seem smaller and the valleys seem shallower and the mountains seem movable for people like that.

THE RELUCTANT HERO

But maybe perhaps you're more typical, and the journey through the valley is not one you take unflinchingly. Usually, the hero shows some hesitation or reticence on this leg of the journey. It is a fact of life. Many of us who embark on a hero's journey spends some time as the reluctant hero.

No wonder, then, that we resonate so deeply with the stories of reluctant heroes. We identify with the tension that King George VI feels in *The King's Speech* when, despite his strong stutter, must overcome his fear of public embarrassment and give a radio address to address the people as the United Kingdom declared war on Nazi Germany at the onset of World War II.

This is why Jack Ryan is such a memorable character that fills the pages of nine Tom Clancy novels and movies and TV shows starring Alec Baldwin, Harrison Ford, Ben Affleck,

Chris Pine, and John Krasinski as the title character. Ryan, an analyst for the CIA, repeatedly faces the choice to go from his desk job into the heat of action—overcoming his reluctance along the way.

Even Superman can be reluctant. In the *Man of Steel* version of his origin story, when Clark Kent finds out about his powers and how he arrived on earth from another planet, his response is reluctance as he asks his adoptive father, "Can I just keep pretending I'm your son?"

I'm sure you can think of countless other examples of the reluctant hero. From Queen Elsa's decision to "let it go" to Frodo Baggins' stops and starts, we see the reluctant hero over and over again.

Why are heroes reluctant? Perhaps it's because they know, or at least sense, the weight and the cost of the call they have just become aware of. As they start to acknowledge the challenge, their knees buckle, and they wonder if they can (or should) embark on the hero's journey.

This is the feeling that many of us have when we first hold the infant whom we are called to parent. Or when we make vows to a new husband or wife. Or when we step onto a campus for the first day of university, or into an office on a new job. These moments take our breath away because they are weighty. And they are weighty because our eyes are opened not just to the path in front of us but to the cost of traveling that path.

Of course, this is nothing new. The Bible tells us many stories of characters who showed this same reluctance. From Moses at the burning bush to Gideon and his fleece, Scripture reminds us that it is natural for us to flinch when we face the Kingdom responsibility of undertaking the hero's journey.

Even Jesus did this before he started the journey to Calvary. "Going a little farther, he fell with his face to the ground and prayed, 'My Father, if it is possible, may this cup be taken from me. Yet not as I will, but as you will.'"[5] This is one of Jesus'

---

5   Matthew 26:39

most human moments, as he confesses his reluctance. And yet, as our perfect example, he chooses not to succumb to the challenge but instead to embrace the call of the hero's journey, the Kingdom responsibility, and the overriding mission for which he had come.

And while Jesus experienced the horror of God the Father turning his face away at Golgotha, we have wonderfully good news in our story—God will always be with us. As God told Joshua before his journey into the Promised Land,

> *After the death of Moses the servant of the Lord,*
> *the Lord said to Joshua son of Nun, Moses' aide: 'Moses*
> *my servant is dead. Now then, you and all these people,*
> *get ready to cross the Jordan River into the land I am*
> *about to give to them—to the Israelites. I will give you*
> *every place where you set your foot, as I promised*
> *Moses. Your territory will extend from the desert to*
> *Lebanon, and from the great river, the Euphrates—all*
> *the Hittite country—to the Mediterranean Sea in the*
> *west. No one will be able to stand against you all the*
> *days of your life. As I was with Moses, so I will be*
> *with you; I will never leave you nor forsake you. Be*
> *strong and courageous, because you will lead these*
> *people to inherit the land I swore to their ancestors to*
> *give them.*
>
> *'Be strong and very courageous. Be careful to obey all*
> *the law my servant Moses gave you; do not turn from*
> *it to the right or to the left, that you may be successful*
> *wherever you go. Keep this Book of the Law always on*
> *your lips; meditate on it day and night, so that you may*
> *be careful to do everything written in it. Then you will*
> *be prosperous and successful. Have I not commanded*
> *you? Be strong and courageous. Do not be afraid; do not*
> *be discouraged, for the Lord your God will be with you*
> *wherever you go.'* [6]

---

6   Joshua 1:1-9

Our Kingdom responsibility always comes with Covenant relationship with God. It is imperative that we communicate this truth to the reluctant heroes in our midst. It is an integral part of acknowledging and ultimately overcoming the challenge before us.

COMMUNICATING TO THE RELUCTANT HERO

What should our stance be to the reluctant heroes in our audience? What should our stance be toward linguistic codes having to do with doubt or uncertainty, or to other voices who hesitated on the path of their hero's journey?

As we saw in the example of Stephen, the way to win a hearing with your audience is to start with a positive stance, not a negative one. This is likewise true when we address the reluctant hero before us.

But is this the stance we typically use with those who are reluctant to undertake the hero's journey God has called them on? Or do we as pastors and leaders default to negative stances like the use of guilt to get people to do evangelism or to go on missions trip or to give money to the church?

You and I both know the answer to that question. Far too often, we as leaders try to pressure or guilt-trip people just to get them moving—without regard to the fact that this movement will likely burn out in short order. We want to see a response, and so we will try every rhetorical trick in the book to get people to raise a hand or walk down the aisle. And then we measure these pressurized gifts or conversions as a sign of our effectiveness—instead of measuring the true fruit of discipleship and mission that comes much further down the line. I often call people to make a physical response to the preached word of God.

But I have found that awakening people to the hero's journey will lead us to communicate in a different way. We will be honest about the challenges, but also show the invitation to fruit. We will talk just as much (if not more) about the covenant relationship with God and with his people along the journey as we will about the responsibility of undertaking the journey.

FROM RELUCTANT TO REALISTIC

The reluctance that people feel along the hero's journey is a natural instinct. Our goal as communicators should not be to squash that instinct—it should be to respond to the instinct in the best way.

The wrong response to the reluctant instinct is to be paralyzed with fear. Rather, we can say that since God is with us, as he was with Joshua, we can be strong and courageous. The Lord is our Shepherd and our Warrior. He fights with us and for us, and he leads us not through the valley of death to the blessing of a "table set in the presence of our enemies." We need not be paralyzed with fear.

So what is the right response to reluctance? To use one of Jesus' memes, it is to "count the cost."

> *"Suppose one of you wants to build a tower. Won't you first sit down and estimate the cost to see if you have enough money to complete it? For if you lay the foundation and are not able to finish it, everyone who sees it will ridicule you, saying, 'This person began to build and wasn't able to finish.'*
>
> *"Or suppose a king is about to go to war against another king. Won't he first sit down and consider whether he is able with ten thousand men to oppose the one coming against him with twenty thousand? If he is not able, he will send a delegation while the other is still a long way off and will ask for terms of peace. In the same way, those of you who do not give up everything you have cannot be my disciples."* [7]

Reluctance is actually a necessary step on the hero's journey.

---

7   Luke 14:28-33

It leads us to count the cost and acknowledge the challenge of the journey before us. It is this kairos moment that leads us to process the call, and repent and believe in a way that we change the trajectory of our lives is changed and we actually go on the hero's journey.[8]

As communicators, we need to help people count the cost and acknowledge the challenge of the hero's journey to which Jesus calls each of us. Taking up the cross isn't easy. It costs us everything.

How many times have Sally and I, and our kids, had to say goodbye to friends and family and all we know to embark on the next season God has for us? Between the five of us, we've moved 130 times (and counting). That's a lot of goodbyes, a lot of starting over, a lot of uncertainty, and a lot of challenge. It is worth it, but it's not easy.

FROM REALISTIC TO RESOLVED

We need to tell people it will be hard. And then we need to tell people that the fruitful bounty at the end of the journey is worth the difficulty.

Likewise, we should tell people that the journey is possible. When God calls us to a particular path, he gives us the grace we need for that path. No matter how big the giants in our way are, the Lord's presence with us assures us the victory.

We need to be friends or maybe even mentors in the valley. To use a Scriptural example, we need to be Joshuas and Calebs.

> *Joshua son of Nun and Caleb son of Jephunneh, who were among those who had explored the land, tore their clothes and said to the entire Israelite assembly, "The land we passed through and explored is exceedingly good. If the Lord is pleased with us, he will lead us into that land, a land flowing with milk and honey, and will*

---

8   This is the language of the learning circle LifeShape. If you're not familiar with it, you may want to learn more in my book *Building a Discipling Culture*.

*give it to us. Only do not rebel against the Lord. And do
not be afraid of the people of the land, because we will
devour them. Their protection is gone, but the Lord is
with us. Do not be afraid of them."* [9]

So when you communicate, stop pretending that the giants
on the journey aren't that big. And keep reminding people that
the land is flowing with milk and honey, and most of all that the
Lord is with us.

Help them count the cost. Help them acknowledge the
challenge. And take a positive stance toward the reluctance
that becomes realism that becomes resolve for the people
who are ready to be awakened to the call of discipleship and
mission in each of their contexts with the gospel God has
given each of them.

SURRENDER IN THE VALLEY

We're on a journey that is beautifully, fully, and perfectly
articulated by the stories in Scripture. Every story in Scripture
follows the same pattern and path, preparing us to understand
the journey that Jesus took on our behalf as he came as
our champion, our hero, to take on enemies that we found
impossible to overcome. He took on those enemies on our
behalf and vanquished them. He established a victory and
then ascended into heaven and scattered the spoils of war, the
gifts of his Spirit, on his people. [10]

This pattern is something Scripture returns to over and over
again. The more familiar that we become with this pattern,
the more familiar we will become with the insights, the
understanding, and specifically the revelation we can find in
Scripture. In doing that we will be prepared and equipped to
take our own journey as the people of God following the Son
of God.

---

9   Numbers 14:6-9

10   See Philippians 2 and Ephesians 4:7-10.

As we have looked at this pattern, we've noted that the journey comes from a familiar world into an unfamiliar world through the darkness of a valley toward the mountain of victory. On this journey, there are things that our mentor wants to give us so that we can overcome the challenges that we will inevitably find in the valley.

God is calling us to victory, but victory is only found through surrender in the valley. There is no victory without surrender. This is the great paradox of the Christian life. Every other kind of victory you can think of seems to suggest that you need to build on victory from victory, but the hero's journey actually requires us to go through on a journey of surrender.[11]

And at the moment of surrender, we admit to ourselves that we need help. At the moment of surrender, our hearts are open to the mentors and friends God sends to the valley to help us. I am very grateful for the friends and mentors he has sent me.

---

11   This subject is fully explained in the life of Jospeh in my book *Covenant and Kingdom: The DNA of the Bible.*

TWELVE

THE CHALLENGE: MENTORS & FRIENDS

Just about every heroic narrative you come across has the steps that we saw in the last chapter. And as we just saw in Paul's story, just about every story has one more thing that happens to lead the hero to fruitfulness and success—the arrival of a guide or a mentor. The mentor helps us on the journey.

After the inciting incident that causes awareness, and the acknowledgement of the true difficulty and challenge of the journey, the mentor helps the hero along the path and ultimately toward fruitfulness. Often, the mentor goes through much of the journey with his or her heroic apprentice.

Think of how Gandalf helps Frodo on the journey to Sauron. Or how Obi-Wan Kenobi helps Luke Skywalker understand the Force. Or how M reins in James Bond's wilder instincts to help him crack the code and solve the mystery.

I'm sure these examples bring to mind countless more for you. These mentors are omnipresent because they are so necessary.

But why are they necessary?

Heroic journeys include challenges expose weaknesses in the protagonist. But the weaknesses that are exposed are dealt with in different ways. They either function as something of an Achilles' heel when we face the antagonist in the story, or they function as a conduit or a corrective when we meet the mentor who guides us, gives us gifts, and takes us to the place of victory.

These two divergent paths show the importance of the mentor. In many examples, the mentor is the one who shows the hero the way to overcome that fatal flaw so that he or she can complete the journey and find fruitfulness at the end.

Here again, Jesus is the model of mentor for us. Think of how he restored Peter after Peter's impetuousness led him to deny Jesus three times.

> When they had finished eating, Jesus said to Simon Peter, "Simon son of John, do you love me more than these?"
>
> "Yes, Lord," he said, "you know that I love you."
>
> Jesus said, "Feed my lambs."
>
> Again Jesus said, "Simon son of John, do you love me?"
>
> He answered, "Yes, Lord, you know that I love you."
>
> Jesus said, "Take care of my sheep."
>
> The third time he said to him, "Simon son of John, do you love me?"
>
> Peter was hurt because Jesus asked him the third time, "Do you love me?" He said, "Lord, you know all things; you know that I love you."

Jesus said, "Feed my sheep. Very truly I tell you, when you were younger you dressed yourself and went where you wanted; but when you are old you will stretch out your hands, and someone else will dress you and lead you where you do not want to go." Jesus said this to indicate the kind of death by which Peter would glorify God. Then he said to him, "Follow me!" [1]

After Jesus ascended to heaven, he sent the Holy Spirit to be our mentor along the hero's journey. Jesus asserted that it is for our good that he returned to heaven:

"But very truly I tell you, it is for your good that I am going away. Unless I go away, the Advocate will not come to you; but if I go, I will send him to you." [2]

This is a pretty outlandish claim when you think about it. This is because we don't have a good understanding of how the Holy Spirit guides us and helps us and leads us.

Jesus teaches that "the Advocate, the Holy Spirit, whom the Father will send in my name, will teach you all things and will remind you of everything I have said to you." [3] And we see in the book of Acts countless examples of the Spirit's leading:

- The Spirit gives courage [4]
- The Spirit gives peacefulness under persecution [5]
- The Spirit gives encouragement [6]
- The Spirit gives specific guidance on what to do (or avoid doing) on the next steps of the journey [7]

---

1   John 21:15-19

2   John 16:7. The paraclete is perhaps better translated as mentor.

3   John 14;26

4   Acts 4:8 and 4:25

5   Acts 7:55

6   Acts 9:31

7   Acts 13:4 and 16:6

I have found these gifts immensely helpful along my journey.

The leading of the Spirit is evident in our decision to leave Greenville and go to Dayton, our current assignment. This has meant leaving a fantastic city, wonderful friends, and our children and grandchildren. Yet we have gotten peace throughout and power for this new work.

I trust that you too have benefited from the work of the Spirit.

Our hero's journey is all about us embracing our mentor, our friend, our sage, our discipler—and in that relationship receiving fresh gifts and seeing new victory. On the journey, our antagonist will undoubtedly try to expose our weaknesses and sins. But these are not fatal flaws, because our mentor, the blessed Holy Spirit, working often through a human agent, will bring you gifts, bring you insights, and bring you an understanding and comfort and encouragement to keep going.

Mentors are valuable because they have been through the valley before. As I already discussed, my personal journey has been like a relay race of hero's journeys—through the valley, to the mountaintop, and back and forth again and again. These trips through the valley mean that I have gained gifts and tools that I can share with others.

That's what mentors do. Mentors are not more heroic than us, or better than us. They're simply more experienced. After a trip

or two or three through the valley, they can share the gifts they have gained to help us. I have been privileged to have two or three of these who have walked with me on the road I was traveling.

We've already talked about how our heroes are broken heroes. The same is true of mentors. The best mentors aren't perfect; they're guides who know the way through the desert because they've already been there themselves. They are broken mentors who have learned from the ultimate mentor, the Holy Spirit, and can share what they have learned.

This is the way God intended it to work. He sends all of us to make disciples because any of us can do it. Anyone can be a mentor because broken mentors can disciple broken heroes. Isn't it amazing that God set it up to work like this?

COMMUNICATORS AS MENTORS

So where do we as communicators fit in as mentors who awaken the hero's journey, working in concert with the Holy Spirit?

This is the spot where we so often stop short as preachers and leaders. I say this with confidence, because I did it.

When I ministered in Brixton Hill in London, our parish experienced incredible growth. It was a great season of fruitfulness—but that fruitfulness didn't last over the long haul. Not that long after I left, the effect of missional communities and cell groups declined.

Looking back, I would now say that we had experienced awakening, but not in-depth discipleship. We had got everyone stirred up, and there was some tremendous fruit, but it didn't sustain over the long run.

Sally and I reflected on this during our time of pruning and abiding in Arkansas. We changed our approach from "Family and Mission" to "Family on Mission," and we realized with the help of our mentor the Holy Spirit that we needed to focus on discipleship when we returned to England to minister in Sheffield.

In Sheffield, as in Brixton Hill, we saw a great deal of awakening. But this time, the awakening sustained. The church has continued to thrive, now more than 20 years after we departed. Discipleship and mission, fueled by awakening, led to continuing conversion.

Discipleship and mission is what people remember from this time. That's what the 3DM movement has focused on ever since. But communication was a key part of this. If you ask people who attended St. Thomas in Sheffield in those days what they remember, many of them will tell you the worship and word on Sundays.

Communication led to awakening. This awakening created a hunger for discipleship and mission, which happened in Huddles. Discipleship and mission happened in the context of family on mission, which we provided through vehicles like Missional Communities.

Each part is important. But it's vital to see how each part works together. Communication starts the awakening, but public communication from the stage is not the method for true discipleship. It can light the spark, but that spark needs the right fuel and the right shelter. I know this not just as a theorist, but as a practitioner who has seen what it takes to go from awakening to conversion through discipleship and mission.

So as a communicator, you need to speak toward awakening. Help people become aware of the hero's journey, acknowledge the challenge of the journey, and awaken to begin the journey.

And then ensure that people have a place where the spark of awakening can be fanned into a flame, with the help of a mentor who can teach these awakened heroes to listen to the Holy Spirit working through kairos moments and act on what God is saying to them. This is what a Huddle does—it provides a context of discipleship where the voice of the Holy Spirit becomes clearer and clearer to the hero, so he or she can move on in the journey.

And as these heroes are discipled by their broken mentors, they will move forward into mission. This happens most effectively when they have a family around them—whether a nuclear family on mission, or a missional community that is like a family. This group that is small enough to care but large enough to dare can claim new territory for the kingdom of God, and lead to new awakening and deepening conversion. This is the fruit God calls us to produce.

It starts with awakening, which happens when a communicator like you brings your gospel into your context to awaken the heroes before you. Let us all pray that God gives all of us this kind of fruit through our communication.

As we surrender in the valley to the mentor who brings us the necessary gifts, the mentor will bring us an understanding of how a call has brought us here. He will reveal to us how the message that we carry, that we show and that we say, is a message not only for those that we encounter, but one that so harbors the faith that it is actually the means by which the mountains move.

To escape the valley, we need to see the mountains move. How do mountains move? They move by faith. How do we have faith? Faith comes from hearing. Faith comes from hearing the message, and the message is heard through the word of Christ. Jesus works on us in the valley so that the message that we carry, our gospel, is both a window into the bigger gospel and a window into hearts. It becomes a portal into our hearts by which God is able to speak to us again and again.

Here's an example from my wife Sally. She's walked through the landscape of her life. She's been on many heroic missionary journeys. We've traveled together in this life of mission for decades. She was the very first Christian I ever met of my own age. Everybody else was just old people. Then one day the pastor said to me, "You do realize there are young people that go to this church?" I said, "Really? I've never seen them. They're all old people." He said, "Well, they go to the evening service, and they have a thing called koinonia on a

Saturday night." I said, "Koinonia. What's that?" He said, "It's a Greek word for fellowship." I didn't realize it. I was only a new Christian. I didn't realize that you couldn't have cool things unless they were with a Greek name.

I went along and I tied up my bike outside on the lamppost and went into the church hall. All the kids were on the stage sitting in a circle. It looked like a scene from the video "Let It Be." They're all sitting around on cushions and playing guitars and looking groovy.

One of those young people separated herself from the crowd. She had jet-black curly hair. She was wearing a white and blue hooped long sleeve t-shirt, a pair of Lee jeans, and clogs, which were the fashion then. The clogs were supposed to go underneath the bell bottoms of your jeans. She said, "Hello. My name's Sally." I immediately recognized the smile and these amazing, marbly eyes and thought, "What a lucky chap I am." Then she introduced me to her boyfriend.

All through the years we've known each other as friends, and then in courtship and then in marriage, and as young parents, and, whatever we are now—spiritual grandparents or old people. Sally has navigated her own journey alongside me. We've had a journey together and we've had journey with the Lord that has been individual. Her journey has brought home to her over and over again the faithfulness of God.

As I mentioned earlier, the faithfulness of God is Sally's gospel. It is a window into the larger gospel, because once you understand faithfulness, you understand the whole gospel from the point of view of faithfulness. And faithfulness functions as faith in Sally's heart, because she hears the message over and over again. My experience is that for faith to grow in the heart of a believer, you need to hear the message over and over, and it's you that needs to speak to yourself the message.

I can hear her saying to the girls as they grew up saying, "God is faithful." I can hear her in her huddles with people all around the world saying, "God is faithful." As she's sharing her gospel, she is sharing the message with herself, and her faith becomes clearer. I don't know whether it grows. I don't think it needs to. All we need is a mustard seed. I do think it becomes clearer. When we face unassailable obstacles, she looks at the mountain, and she says, "God is faithful." Imagine the impact of those words repeated over multiple years on the hearts of our kids as they faced the challenge of moving across the Atlantic or making new friends once again or in one of the countless other valleys we have faced. You begin to hear this rumbling and you being to hear this moving, and before you know it, despite the challenge of the valley, the mountain's gone and your journey can continue.

In the valley, the mentor brings us the message, as Sally has done for our kids and so many more. If you listen to the message that has changed you, it will be the means by which you receive the faith to move the mountains that confront you.

MENTORS AND THEIR VALLEYS

Our time in the valley in fact often parallels our mentor's time in the valley. They are not on the same journey as us, but our descent in the valley syncs up with theirs. When this happens, we can actually watch the way they journey through the valley and learn by observing and imitating what they do.

We see an example of this happen in the book of Judges, where a hero named Barak relies on his mentor Deborah to conquer both the enemy of the Canaanite army and his enemy within.

The Bible doesn't give us a lot of background on Deborah's previous heroic journeys—it simply tells us that Deborah "was leading Israel at that time."[8] But this simple statement belies a stark reality of what must have happened in Deborah's past to make her a female judge in Israel's history. We don't know precisely what her journey was, but we can safely assume that she had been on a heroic journey by this point.

8   Judges 4:4

So Deborah calls Barak to lead Israel's military against the armies of Canaan. And Barak says he can't do it without her.

> She sent for Barak son of Abinoam from Kedesh in Naphtali and said to him, "The Lord, the God of Israel, commands you: 'Go, take with you ten thousand men of Naphtali and Zebulun and lead them up to Mount Tabor. I will lead Sisera, the commander of Jabin's army, with his chariots and his troops to the Kishon River and give him into your hands.'"
>
> Barak said to her, "If you go with me, I will go; but if you don't go with me, I won't go."
>
> "Certainly I will go with you," said Deborah. "But because of the course you are taking, the honor will not be yours, for the Lord will deliver Sisera into the hands of a woman." So Deborah went with Barak to Kedesh. There Barak summoned Zebulun and Naphtali, and ten thousand men went up under his command. Deborah also went up with him.[9]

Deborah was Barak's mentor, and she gave the command for Barak to send the Israelites to the Kishon River to attack Sisera's army. When he does, Sisera flees, only to fall into the hands of Jael, who killed Sisera. It was the turning point that allowed the Israelites to ultimately destroy the reign of Jabin king of Canaan. And then "the land had peace for forty years."[10]

The blessings of the hero's journey for Barak would never have been realized without Deborah's simultaneous journey (as well as her previous journeys). But thanks to her continued commitment to be both hero and mentor, she was able to lead Israel to victory and a generation of peace in the land.

---

9   Judges 4:6-10

10   Judges 5:31

As mentor, Deborah did not avoid the valley. She descended again so she could be a mentor to Barak, and she emerged with her people as a hero once more. Even her song found in Judges 5 is a form of continued mentorship—sharing what God had done, and how he is with us in the valley time after time.

FRIENDS IN THE VALLEY

What else happens in the valley? One of the patterns you discover as you look at the hero's journey all the way through Scripture, and again in the life of Jesus, is that in the valley you not only receive skills and gifts from the mentor but you also receive help and encouragement from friends and allies.

Let's look at some examples.

David wrestles with the reality that, unless God does something amazing, he'll never be king, even though Samuel, the great man of God, has told him that that's what he'll be one day. He wrestles even though the best friend that he's ever had, Jonathan, the son of the king, tells him that he'll be king one day. In the midst of the reflection in the valley, God sends him brothers and his friends, and they function together as oikos.[11]

Jesus comes to Nazareth and speaks to his family, his relatives, the community in which he has been raised for 30 years, where he gained notoriety as a godly man, and he tells them that the Spirit of the Lord is upon him for the breakthrough of God's kingdom. They're tremendously excited until he says, "And it's for the sinners as well." It's for all of the people that, up until now, you thought were excluded from God's grace. They begin to become aggressive toward him, and then violent toward him, and they take him to the cliff. And here's the shocking thing: There's no mention of Mary holding on to the cloak of Jesus and saying, "Don't touch my boy." There's no defensive ring among his brothers who stand to protect him. Everyone rejects him.

11   Care of Adullum

Where does Jesus go? He has been sent by the Father to form a family. The natural place to go is to his hometown. Of course, he has set aside his omniscience. He has set aside his omnipotence. He's set aside the glories of heaven and come as a servant among us, listening to the words of the Spirit, seeing what his Father's doing, so that he can be our model, our mentor, our master. Jesus has to come to an understanding that his own family and hometown are not the place where he will find friends and allies for his hero's journey. So he goes and finds them in Capernaum. Jesus needed friends who became family, and that means that you do too. All of us need friends and family on our hero's journey. [12]

FINDING MENTORS AND FRIENDS

Let's return to thinking about Paul's journey as a hero. And let's begin with the truth that what he *doesn't* say in his letters is often what is so interesting. He doesn't tell us that when he was beaten five times with the 40 lashes minus one that this means he was excommunicated from five synagogues. This is hugely important for us to understand. When he says that he got 39 lashes from the Jews, he's talking about the highest measure of punishment that the court of a synagogue can execute upon a convicted man. He got this punishment five times! We all know the horror and the terror of the 39 lashes. For a man to even be alive after all this is amazing.

All of the stories external to the Bible that share with us the collective memory of the early church tell us that Paul was physically a broken man by the time that Barnabas came to find him. He spent a decade in what appears to be largely fruitless ministry. There's no indication that there was any fruit from Paul's early work. He had been out on the open sea and somehow had a shipwreck, because the shipwreck that he tells us that he suffered in Malta happens much later. He's been traveling the world. He's been going to his hometown where the apostles in Jerusalem sent him. He's gone to his

---

12   You can find a more complete rendering of this story in the book *Family on Mission* by my wife Sally and me.

home community and to successive synagogues and shared the story of Jesus, and has not just been rejected but also beaten within an inch of his life and excommunicated from that community. What that means is this: His family considers him dead, and his wife divorces him because he no longer is alive.

You may be asking, "Well, are you sure he's married?" If he weren't married, he would have been the only Jewish male in the whole of Jewish history who would have been given the responsibility of taking the commission of the chief priest to persecute the sect called Christians. Nobody at that time would have been given that responsibility without first being married and having a family. It would never, ever happen. Paul actually indicates that he has a wife. He talks about how the other apostles take their wives along,[13] but he doesn't say that he doesn't have a wife. He simply says that he doesn't do that. I think the reason he doesn't do that is because his family has so rejected him that it's impossible for his family to even connect with him. There is a nephew that comes and offers him help and succor when he's in prison in Caesarea, and there are a couple of indications in the personal comments at the ends of his letters that perhaps some of his family have come to faith, but that's the only confirmation of any continued family connection. There's no indication that the family who were part of the synagogue that excommunicated him were ever able to embrace him again.

Think about this for a minute. The stories external to the Scriptures tell us that the memory of the church is that Barnabas came to look for Saul in the place that he and the apostles have sent him, his home in Tarsus, but couldn't find him. Barnabas is a Levite of unusual capacity and high status in the Jewish community, so nobody's going to cross him. When he asked questions about this renegade Paul, people would assume he was asking for the same reason that they would and would try to help. But Barnabas can't find him anywhere. He goes from place to place, synagogue to synagogue, and finally finds that Saul (he's still using that

---

13   1 Corinthians 9:5

name) is hiding in the Taurus Mountains in a cave, afraid for his life.

Barnabas finds Saul there, and this once vital zealot who pursued Christians to their death, who met Jesus on the road to Damascus, is now so covered in scar tissue that he cannot straighten his back. He has been beaten so many times that the same thing happens to his body that happens to anyone who has suffered that mistreatment. His legs become bandy. The joints and the muscles don't work in the way they used to do. This Quasimodo kind of figure is to become the apostle of the New Testament. But at the point Barnabas found him, Saul was completely alone.

When Barnabas found Saul, he tells him, "It's happening. The thing that Jesus said to you on the road to Damascus is actually happening. Thousands of Gentiles are coming under the sound of the gospel. There's a harvest. Will you join me?"

Saul does. He spends his first missionary journey (the next lap of his hero's journey) hearing the call to go on mission. He has Barnabas as his mentor. They go to Barnabas' hometown, because (as you'll remember) when you have a mission, you always start with your friends and family. So they go to Cyprus and preach in all of the synagogues in Cyprus.

In the middle of Cyprus, it's apparent that Saul is supposed to be the leader because he does things like preach to the governor and blind his magician. He obviously has the moxie. Barnabas hands over the torch of leadership, and Saul takes the name of Paul because the first governor is Sergius Paulus. Paul is now going to carry that name as an indicator of the fulfillment of the first promise that Jesus made to him—that the governors and kings of the Gentiles will hear the gospel. Paul was probably also a name that was given to him as a boy. He is from a high-ranking family who were Roman citizens, and such families gave numerous names to their children. Saul was a name that indicated his Jewish heritage. Paul was a name that indicated his status within the Roman Empire. Sergius Paulus has just become a believer, and so Saul becomes Paul, and the follower becomes the leader.

Paul goes to territory that he understands, the coastline of what is now modern day Turkey. It's just outside of his "Jerusalem and Judea," but he can't go to his Jerusalem and Judea because every synagogue that he had gone to had excommunicated him. He goes to his "Samaria," which is called Pamphylia. The big city in Pamphylia is called Perga. If you go to Perga, it's like stepping onto the set of *The Lord of the Rings*, because there is this amazing noble Roman city with great hippodromes and gladiatorial arenas. As you look towards Galatia, there is the jagged tooth line of the mountains waiting to devour you. In those mountains, live the rebellious Celts, whom no empire can ever subjugate. They've given their name as Gauls to the region of Galatia.

These are people who will not bow the knee. Almost the entire population in this area is enslaved. In most parts of the Roman Empire, 50 percent of the population is enslaved. In Galatia it's 90 percent. There's no hope if you live there. So this people runs away and become bands of brigands in the mountains. If you travel through those mountains unguarded and unwatched by the Roman legions that crisscross that region, you will die. You will be beaten, you will be stripped, you will be left for dead on the side of the road, and you will not get out. Everybody knows it. John Mark, who's with Barnabas and Paul, decides that he's going home to mom instead. He has seen these mountains and questioned why anybody would go there. He rejects his hero's journey at this stage, but he will rejoin it later in life.

Paul completes his first missionary journey, and then has a bit of a confrontation with Peter in Antioch. Peter and Paul go to Jerusalem to hear the ruling of the apostles and the elders that the Gentiles do not need to become Jews first so that they can follow Jesus. They can follow Jesus and receive the grace of Jesus without becoming Jewish. The "Council of Jerusalem" writes a letter affirming these things, and Paul and Barnabas return to Antioch with much rejoicing.

Paul wants to take the letter from Jerusalem to all the churches that are being troubled by these teachers and preachers insisting on circumcision to tell them they're OK.

Barnabas wants to take John Mark along, but Paul refuses. They have a sharp disagreement. So Paul takes Silas, a prophet from Jerusalem, with him, while Barnabas takes John Mark and goes back to Cyprus. Paul goes back into the Taurus Mountains where Barnabas found him, through the Cilician gates, into Galatia, and onto the west.[14]

As they travel west, Paul wants to go to the great city of Ephesus in the region called Asia in the midst of Asia Minor, but the Holy Spirit prevents them. Paul then tries to Bithynia in the north by the Black Sea, but the spirit of Jesus prevents them again.[15] They stay on the road and travel to a place locally known as Alexandria, because that's where Alexander the Great landed with his great army that would conquer the world. The city is littered with images of Alexander. Just up the road is ancient Troy. The Romans call it Troas. There, Luke joins them. We know he joins them because in the book of Acts the account of this journey becomes the first person plural at this point. (We did this. We did that.)

Paul has also picked up Timothy along the way, so he has Timothy and Silas and Luke with him. One night, Paul has a dream of a Macedonian man saying, "Come over and help us." Little did Paul know that Jesus was sending him an image of a Macedonian man (who probably looked like the Alexander the Great images he was seeing everywhere around town) to invite him into Europe for the first time. Little did Paul know that in Europe, he would receive the method that would carry the gospel for the next 250 years in the midst of persecution. Little did he know that the Roman Empire would become 50 percent Christian despite a great period of persecution, because of the thing that he would discover at his first location in Europe. Paul just knew where he needed to go next.

The next morning, Paul and his group got a boat that takes them into Europe via Samothrace, which is a little island in the middle of the Aegean Sea. They dock at Neapolis, which is the first port in Greece they encounter. Then they travel to

---

14   Acts 15:41

15   Acts 16:7

the Roman city of Philippi. It's the principal city of the region. Not coincidentally, it's named after the father of Alexander the Great.

THE TURNING POINT IN PHILIPPI

Philippi is the place where Brutus fell on his sword when he fought the great battle against Octavian, who would become Caesar Augustus. This place is so soaked in the military history of Rome that when Roman soldiers want a little piece of land to call their own upon retiring, they always ask for Philippi. Philippi is a Latin-speaking city with no synagogue, full of soldiers and old soldiers. If you go there, it's amazing, because it's nothing but gaming halls and baths and restaurants. Why? It's full of soldiers who have disposable incomes. And part of this is that many have wives who want nice clothes, so there's a lot of fashion in Philippi.

So it's no surprise that one of the fashionistas living there meets Paul and his team. She's called Lydia, from Thyatira, a place known for high fashion because they make purple cloth. Purple cloth is important because it's the color of imperial Rome. If you're going to have an evening gown, you're going to want it to be purple.

Lydia brought her operation to Philippi because there's lots of money. She brings along her models, and she is the head of a household, her oikos, which is mostly populated by women. Within the oikos, women were the leaders of the home. Men were the leaders of the oikos in public life, but the man did not attempt to lead the oikos inside the home. The woman was raised to be the manager of the oikos and to engineer this incredibly complex system that was the center of social life, education, healing, politics, and commerce. The man oversaw the business of the oikos, which was what the oikos did as its mission. The woman led the ministry of the oikos. But in Lydia's case, a woman led not only the ministry of the oikos but also the mission. This was quite unusual, and it tells us that Lydia was obviously a formidable woman.

Lydia is a God fearer. Many women who looked at paganism and the way they were demeaned and subjugated within Greek and Roman society searched for an alternative, and in Judaism they found an understanding that men and women were created equal. So it was attractive for them to embrace the law of the Old Testament and the ways of the Jewish people.

Lydia and her oikos worshipped wherever they could as God fearers, but in Philippi there is no synagogue. So they gathered by a flowing river so that they could take part in the ritual ablutions of the Jews that required running water. Paul knew to look for a group of praying people by a river, and he found a place of prayer populated with Lydia and some women. Paul shared the gospel with her, and she became a Christian. She said this, "If you count me worthy." That's a big statement. If you count me as a woman, a Gentile, a person from outside of your world, as worthy, of receiving the gospel that you shared with us today, then come and stay in our oikos.[16]

The young guys who are with Paul must have been thinking, "Awesome. The place is full of supermodels. Why wouldn't you want to go and stay there? Have you seen those girls?" But what is Paul to do as the apostle? He knows what Jesus said about finding a person of peace. He says they've got to like you, they've got to listen to you, and they've got to serve you. She seems to check those boxes. But Paul expected to find a he, and Lydia is clearly a she. Very insightfully, Luke records that Lydia "persuaded us." What a formidable woman.

This is a key moment, because from that point on, Paul was released from going to the synagogue as his principal strategy. When he went to Corinth, he joined the oikos of Priscilla and Aquila, an oikos that bears the name of the woman first. This transformed the way he did ministry by eliminating the sting of excommunication. As long as he could find an oikos, he had a foothold for his missionary work.

---

16   Acts 16:15

THE POWER OF OIKOS

When Paul goes to Ephesus, he does the greatest work of his life. It comes time to say farewell, and he gathers the elders on the beach at Miletus and says something like, "You know the ministry that I did among you. You know how I worked with these hands to support myself, and you know the ministry that I did in public (in the Hall of Tyrannus and house to house)." In other words, Paul worked in the oikos, and they went to the Hall of Tyrannus for the big-scale teaching.[17]

Rodney Stark, the great social historian of the New Testament, talks about how the oikos was the principal reason why the church of Jesus, the movement of Jesus, went from a small insignificant group, to become 50 percent of the Roman empire during 250 years of persecution.[18]

As you encounter the challenges that inevitably come on your hero's journey, you need to answer a key question: Who's your oikos?

You cannot complete your hero's journey alone. Do you know how I know that? Even Jesus on the cross had people gathered to help and support him. In fact, around the cross a new oikos was formed. Before Jesus breathed his last, he looked at his mother and the dearest of disciples and said, "Mother, here is your son. Son, here is your mother."[19]

Speaking of Ephesus, after Paul had established the most important church for the next 400 years and had sent his assistant Timothy to lead it, and after both had died in different waves of persecution, John the apostle as an old man comes to Ephesus with an even older lady called Mary. She's buried there. I've seen her grave. Mary and John were always oikos.

You can't do the hero's journey without your oikos. It's not possible. You need the message that will give you faith to

---

17   Acts 20:13 and following

18   Rodney Stark, *The Rise of Christianity* (Princeton: Princeton University Press, 1997).

19   John 19:26-27

move the mountains, but you need your family, that usually start as friends, to help you go through the valley. I hope that by hearing Paul's journey and reflecting on that journey that Jesus has you on, you're prepared today to take a fresh stab at developing an oikos. God is calling you into a family, and in that family, that family of heroes, you'll complete the journey and share the spoils of victory with many.

BEYOND THE CHALLENGE OF THE VALLEY

The challenge along the hero's journey is real, and it is difficult. It may make you question your call and become a reluctant hero.

But God does not leave you alone in the valley. He sends you into the valley with the message of your gospel. He sends the Holy Spirit and other mentors into the valley with gifts to help you move beyond the valley. He even provides friends who become like family to become an oikos that helps you process your call and overcome the challenge, as you help others do the same. And through the process, he helps you gain the tools and skills you will need to ascend out of the valley and complete the journey.

Now you are moving toward the completion of your hero's journey. You are drawing ever closer to awakening in your life and the lives around you.

THIRTEEN

THE COMPLETION OF THE HERO'S JOURNEY

Miraculous Bounties to Share
The Completion of Paul's Journey
Really Good News
Awakening Erupts

The hero's journey that we're on in our lives is first revealed to us in the life of Jesus, a life that is explained and shown to us in the models and qualifiers of all of the other heroes in scripture. From these examples, we see that the hero's journey begins with a call, continues with a particular challenge, and finishes with a completion expressed in multiple blessings.

The call—that is obviously from God—takes us across the threshold and sends us on mission. As we've seen, the mission faces challenges along the way, and in the midst of that challenge, we grasp the depth of the message—the window into the gospel to share with the world. We learn how to journey through the valley with our friends and allies who become our family, and we receive from our mentor spiritual gifts and wisdom that help us in the valley and beyond.

Our mentor meets us in the journey and encourages us in the valley. As a result, we learn the purpose, the value, and the importance of the message that we carry, the people that we

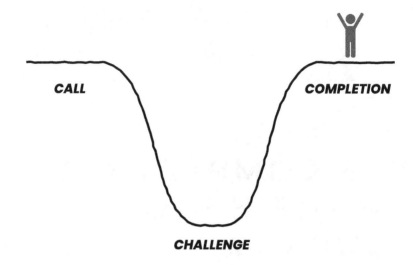

walk with, and the God who can change things. In other words, the completion of the journey comes with evidence of the blessings we have received—reflected in our gospel and the methods we have learned along the way.

We see the joy and blessings of completion most of all in the journey of Jesus, who is exalted by the God the Father[1] and now sits at the right hand of the Father. We see the same journey in the disciple John, who at the end of his journey (while he is still in captivity on the Isle of Patmos) receives the gift of a Revelation that has blessed all Christ followers to this day.

So what blessings are showered upon us by the Lord Jesus? What are our spoils of war? Paul explains some of the most important in his letter to Christians in Ephesus as he talks about how Jesus descended and then ascended, and then gave the church the blessings of fivefold ministry.

> But to each one of us grace has been given as Christ apportioned it. This is why it says:

---

1 Philippians 2:9

"When he ascended on high,
he took many captives
and gave gifts to his people."

(What does "he ascended" mean except that he also
descended to the lower, earthly regions? He who
descended is the very one who ascended higher than
all the heavens, in order to fill the whole universe.) So
Christ himself gave the apostles, the prophets, the
evangelists, the pastors and teachers, to equip
his people for works of service, so that the body of
Christ may be built up until we all reach unity in the faith
and in the knowledge of the Son of God and become
mature, attaining to the whole measure of the fullness of
Christ.

Then we will no longer be infants, tossed back and forth
by the waves, and blown here and there by every wind
of teaching and by the cunning and craftiness of people
in their deceitful scheming. Instead, speaking the truth
in love, we will grow to become in every respect the
mature body of him who is the head, that is, Christ. From
him the whole body, joined and held together by every
supporting ligament, grows and builds itself up in
love, as each part does its work. [2]

The fivefold ministries of apostles, prophets, evangelists, shepherds, and teachers are a stirring examples of the blessings God gives us as Jesus completes the journey.[3] There are other blessings like the many gifts of the Spirit articulated in the New Testament.

MIRACULOUS BOUNTIES TO SHARE

When Jesus sent out the 12 disciples in the middle of his ministry, he gave a wonderful description of what disciples

---

2   Ephesians 4:7-16

3   You can find more information on the fivefold ministry in chapter eleven of the latest edition of *Building a Discipling Culture.*

should do as they go out. In this description, we discover more of the gifts God gives us on the hero's journey, and we discover what Jesus intends for us to do with them.

> *"As you go, proclaim this message: 'The kingdom of heaven has come near.' Heal the sick, raise the dead, cleanse those who have leprosy, drive out demons. Freely you have received; freely give. Do not get any gold or silver or copper to take with you in your belts— no bag for the journey or extra shirt or sandals or a staff, for the worker is worth his keep."* [4]

These instructions can only go to someone who has been on a hero's journey, because they call us to share the miraculous bounties we have received. Once we are familiar with the topography of the hero's journey, we know about the gifts that God gives us at the end, and we can share those gifts with others.

The thing that will keep us wanting to go on hero's journeys, both journeys of our own and journeys on which we are mentors, is gratitude over the bounties God has given us. The scale of his grace and goodness is grand enough to compel us to give what we have received to others. We can give these bounties away and expect that we will receive gifts from God again. He is a gracious God who loves us--why would he not continue to give us the things necessary for life on the hero's journey?

The completion of the journey comes as we give away what we have received. God will always give more, and so freely you have received, and freely you should give.

THE COMPLETION OF PAUL'S JOURNEY

Now that we have an encouraging picture of the blessings that God gives us to share at the end of the journey, let's look

---

4   Matthew 10:7-10

in more detail at Paul's life to see what the completion of the journey looks like. We've seen how Paul learned from Lydia in Philippi about the key to the evangelization of the Roman Empire through the Greco-Roman oikos. This extended family became the cornerstone of the New Testament church. Having learned this enormously important insight, Paul continues through the cities of Macedonia, through Thessalonica down through Berea.

Paul is opposed along the way. He's sent by the leaders of that region to Athens. There, he struggles with the idolatry of the city and speaks in the agora (marketplace) after having first shared his concern in the synagogue. As he speaks, the philosophers of the day, the stoics and the epicureans tell him he needs to speak to the city council. With the backdrop of the Athenian Acropolis right behind him, he stands on Mars Hill in the city council buildings called the Areopagus, and there shares the message in a contextualized way that Greek people understand. A few come to know the Lord even in that hard-beaten, strange, and distant place that is so disconnected from the gospel.

Then Paul goes to Corinth, which is home to tens of thousands of Jews who have been expelled from Rome by the emperor Claudius. This happened after disturbances in Rome caused by a man called Chrestus[5] Suetonius. A Roman historian tells us that this disturbance was so great that Claudius decided that the whole Jewish population of Rome was to be expelled—maybe 200,000 people. Rome was the largest city the world had ever seen, as many as a million people filled the streets. Maybe a quarter of the population was Jewish. This was a massive number of people thus scattered to the four winds. Of course, if you're Jewish, the principal place that you want to return to is the homeland, and so you journey east.

If you journey east, then all of the ships bring you to Corinth and Cenchrea, two cities separated by an isthmus of land nine kilometers wide. The ships are unloaded in Corinth. They

---

5   Most historians believe that Chrestus is actually "Christus," meaning that the disturbance is about Jesus.

are put on rollers and pushed for the nine miles until they reach Cenchrea, and then their cargo is put back into the boat and they're sent on their way. Of course, this means that the journey is delayed in the precincts of Corinth, and so a huge refugee camp arises. Refugees need tents. Priscilla and Aquila lead a household of tentmakers. Paul is a tentmaker and joins the oikos of this believers while his team is still in northern Greece.

Paul hears news that Silas and Timothy will be joining him. When they arrive, they bring a great gift from the church in Philippi, a gift so large that Paul is released from making tents and commits himself entirely to the preaching of the gospel in the city of Corinth. The synagogue listens attentively at first but then become obstinate and opposed the message of Jesus. So Paul, who's not one to hide his light under a bushel, moves next door to the house of a man named Titius Justus. He establishes his oikos there. The synagogue leader, Chrestus Crispus, becomes a Christian. After all this happens, Jesus meets Paul in a vision in the night.

Why? The opposition to Paul has been growing as he's journeyed through the peninsula of Greece. No doubt, the memories of Paul's sufferings have also come back to him. How many times has he suffered the 39 lashes? How many times has he been beaten? How many times has he been persecuted?

So Jesus comes to Paul and tells him, "Fear not. There are many people that I have in this city, and none of them will touch you." So Paul continues for 18 months. Toward the end of that time, the opposition grows to the extent that the Jewish leadership of the city dragged Paul before the Governor Gallio. But Gallio doesn't even want to listen to them. He throws out the charges and throws all of the Jewish leadership out of his courtroom. Sosthenes, the leader of the synagogue, is even beaten in the streets by the people who have been dishonored by the governor.

Sosthenes clearly has a kairos moment, because just in a few years' time, he goes to Paul in Ephesus and tells him the news that the church is in trouble in Corinth. This indicates that by this point, Sosthenes has become a Christian. In fact, together with Paul, Sosthenes writes the letter we know as 1 Corinthians.

Paul clearly has something in his heart that he needs to talk to the Lord about. Is this going to be the pattern of his heroic journey? Will every missionary journey be a hero's journey where he enters into the valley of trial and faces pain and persecution at every step? We know something was up because Paul shaves all the hair off his body. This probably seems a little strange, but it's quite meaningful.

Note here that Paul is ethnically still a Jew. If a Jew wants to find out something from the Lord, then from his culture and from his ethnic origin, he knows that the Nazarite vow is the way to go. The Nazarite vow means that you eschew all pleasures—you choose not to drink alcohol and you have a simple vegetarian diet. You also shave all of the hair off your body and put the hair in a bag. That bag with that hair represents your life. You take that bag to Jerusalem and give it to a priest, and he puts it in the fires of sacrifice.

In fact, the next time Paul comes to Corinth, he writes a letter that will be known as the Epistle to the Romans, and in this letter he tells them to offer themselves as living sacrifices. We know what memory he was bringing to mind now, don't we?

It begs a question: What could you do, and how could it bring awakening to others if you embraced the journey?

Paul leaves Corinth with Priscilla and Aquila and heads for Jerusalem. The great port of Israel is Caesarea. The ships in those days kept very close to the coastline because nobody had GPS, and they wanted to make sure that they had a port close at hand. As they travel up the coast of Greece and then along the coast of what we now know as Turkey, Paul pulls in at Ephesus, and there is an audience for the gospel there. So Paul leaves Priscilla and Aquila in Ephesus and continues along his way.

REALLY GOOD NEWS

As we saw earlier, Paul asked the Lord three times to take the thorn from his flesh. Christians have speculated for years what the thorn is, but if you read your Bible, there's really no question. The Bible tells us what the thorns in the flesh are. God told Joshua that if he did not remove the Canaanites from the land, they would be a thorn in your flesh.[6] Thorns in your flesh are people. We would call then pains in the neck. It's not a complex exposition.

So the thorns in Paul's flesh are these Judaizers who have pursued him all through his hero's journey. They have been the antagonists raised up by Satan to spoil Paul's work, unsettle the churches that he's planted, and tell the Gentile Christians that they first must become Jews. Paul wants to be rid of them, so he asks God to remove these thorns from his flesh. Paul, in the tradition of his fathers, a tradition even represented by Jesus himself, prays three times. In moments of greatest need, a Jewish woman or man would pray three times, as Jesus did in the garden of Gethsemane. And Paul writes to the Corinthians about how three times he asked the Lord, and the Lord said no.

Instead of saying yes, the Lord tells Paul something like this:

"My grace, which is the message of your life, is enough. The message I've given you enough. You don't need any more than the message I've given you. The window into the gospel is a big enough window, and when it settles in your heart, it will produce all the faith that you need to move any mountain that's in your way. But I'm not going to remove the thorns in your flesh because my grace is sufficient. My power is completed, made mature, perfected in the place where you feel most weak. That's because in the place where you feel most weak, what you need is the message that fills the gap made by your weakness.

"My grace is enough for you. When you're weak, you're going to be strong. Because when you're weak, you're going to go

---

6   Numbers 33:55 and Joshua 23:15

back to your message and you're going to realize that that word is what fills the gap, because that message is the good news to your bad news. Good news is only good news in relation to bad news. Unless you have bad news, you don't even know what good news is. But when there's a weakness in your life, and it's bad news, and because it's bad news, you know where the good news is needed."

AWAKENING ERUPTS

Paul arrives in Caesarea and goes up to greet the church. Whenever you see the phrase "goes up" in the scriptures, it always refers to a journey to Jerusalem. So Paul goes up to greet the church in Jerusalem. In Jerusalem, he takes his little bag of hair and gives it to a priest, and the priest throws it into the fires of sacrifice. Paul prays his prayer and hears his answer, and then makes his journey back home to Antioch. There he decides that there's another missionary journey ordained for him.

Last time, he wanted to go to Ephesus, but the spirit of Jesus wouldn't allow him. This time, he senses he will, because he's left Priscilla and Aquila there and they're already preparing the ground. By the time he gets to Ephesus, there is a mini-Pentecost. Paul prays for some people who only know the baptism of John, and they speak in tongues as the spirit falls. Then Paul enters the synagogue.

> Paul entered the synagogue and spoke boldly there for three months, arguing persuasively about the kingdom of God. But some of them became obstinate; they refused to believe and publicly maligned the Way. So Paul left them. He took the disciples with him and had discussions daily in the lecture hall of Tyrannus.[7]

The lecture hall of Tyrannus was a large public space where they could enjoy the gathering and celebration of worship

7   Acts 19:8-9

of God and the public proclamation of the gospel. We have already seen how Paul met elders of the church of Ephesus on the beach at Miletus to avoid a kerfuffle. There, he reminded them how he worked with his hands and shared with them the whole counsel of God in public in the hall of Tyrannus and from oikos to oikos.

This went on for two years, so all the Jews and Greeks who lived in the province of Asia heard the word of the Lord. Did you catch that? Paul came to Ephesus and became a tentmaker. It was a full-time job! Yet through Paul God plants the most important church for the next 400 years. He awakens thousands of people while he's working as a tentmaker and then speaking during siesta hours.

In the Authorized Version, we find a marginal note made by one of the scribes who copied these texts hundreds and hundreds of years ago. This note tells us that Paul spoke between noon and 4 p.m. Paul began his work making tents as the sun rose. At midday, during the siesta time, when everyone else sleeps, Paul preached at the hall of Tyrannus. Nobody's there because it's the siesta. Then around 4 p.m., Paul went back to work.

This means that Paul has no opportunity to plant the seven churches mentioned in Revelation during his time in Ephesus. He has no opportunity to plant the church in Hierapolis mentioned in Colossians. He has no time to plant the church in Colossae. In fact, he says was planted by Epaphras, whom he had sent to Colossae while he was in Ephesus. Without Paul appearing in person, nine churches are planted in two and a half years. These churches are so important that some of them continued into the 20th century. This movement awakened during Paul's spare time.

How is this possible? Because something had happened to Paul in Jerusalem. Finally, he got to the point of embracing all the frustration, all the difficulty, and all the weakness. He decided that that gospel that Jesus had revealed to him on the road to Damascus was enough.

He was not going to advance anything by his human striving, and so he was going to rest in the knowledge that the message that had received was a good enough message to change the world. He embraced his weakness, he embraced the difficulties, and God did everything else.

The Bible tells us that "God did extraordinary miracles through Paul."[8] That's an expression found nowhere else in the Bible. It's the only place where the word extraordinary is attached to miracle. There are lots of miracles in the Bible, but only one place where extraordinary is attached. It happens in Ephesus after Paul embraced his weakness, and God's power is made perfect in his weakness.

God did extraordinary miracles through Paul, so that even the tools of his trade as a tentmaker were used for ministry. Paul couldn't visit the sick, but he could send the symbols of his identity as a tentmaker—his handkerchiefs, a sweatband around his head, and the big, thick, leather apron he used so that he didn't hurt himself when stitching the canvas together. These items were taken to the sick, and their illnesses were cured and their evil spirits left them.

Who would have ever thought of this? Paul basically sent word that he was tied up in making tents, which is something God had given him to do. To let people know he was praying for them, he sent a symbol like an apron or a sweatband. This was yet another way Paul shared and lived out his message that God's grace was sufficient. He told people although I'm weak and unable to visit you, the Lord's power is enough, and he will do it.

These symbols weren't just there for healing the sick. They also were there as evil spirits were cast out. The way it worked in that day was this: Jewish kids from priestly homes needed money for the summer holidays, and so they got summer jobs as exorcists. The reason they were able to do it was because the priests could read the Hebrew Scriptures. When they read the Hebrew Scriptures, whenever they came to the word

---

8   Acts 19:11

Yahweh, they would replace it with the word Adonai, because the word was too holy for anyone else to hear. So no one knew the name of God but the priests. The priests came in and spoke the name of God over the person who was demonized, and that person was be delivered.

The seven sons of Sceva, a well-known priest, turned up in Ephesus doing just this. When they arrive, they hear about a well-known demoniac who was quite demonically powerful. They decide to take the contract to cast out this demon as long as they are paid enough. They go in and they say Yahweh, the name of God, but nothing happens. Then they say, "Yahweh and Jesus and all of that stuff that Paul talks about." The demon in the man answers, "Jesus I know, and Paul I know about, but who are you?"[9] Then the man jumps on all seven on them, strips them naked, and drives them through the streets of Ephesus.

Seven pastors running naked and screaming through the streets of Ephesus caused the whole city to move into revival.

> When this became known to the Jews and Greeks living in Ephesus, they were all seized with fear, and the name of the Lord Jesus was held in high honor. Many of those who believed now came and openly confessed what they had done. A number who had practiced sorcery brought their scrolls together and burned them publicly. When they calculated the value of the scrolls, the total came to fifty thousand drachmas. In this way the word of the Lord spread widely and grew in power.[10]

The miraculous bounties that Paul enjoyed here were not for their own sake. They affirmed the gospel God had given Paul.

This is the kind of gospel that you and I need. We need this gospel to apply not only to the people around us but also to us. You and I need this kind of powerful, miraculous message.

---

9   Acts 19:14

10   Acts 19:17-20

And there is good news: unless I'm seriously mistaken, you're at least as broken as I am, and the gospel is what joins up the broken pieces and allows the power to flow.

In the midst of your challenge, all of your external trials are nothing in comparison to the trial that's going on inside your heart right now. But it's right there that the gospel is most importantly applied. The message that God has given you is the message that will connect up the broken pieces of your real life and cause you to be whole and complete and cause the power to be made perfect in your weakness.

When we communicate the message God has given us with content that connects to our specific context, we can see the awakening happen thanks to the miraculous power of the gospel. Only by completing the hero's journey can we discover the power of this type of communication.

So whether you are considering the start of the journey with your call, or persevering through the valley while you look for friends and mentors, or whether you are nearing the completion where you see the fruits of awakening all around, continue on your journey. And as you do, embrace the message that changes us so that we can communicate to others.

FOURTEEN

DEVELOPING A DASHBOARD

Content: Message, Metanarrative, Meme
Context: History, Biography, Stance
Conversation: Call, Challenge, Completion

How do we bring all of these ideas together conceptually as we look for ways to speak to our audiences? My suggestion is that we use a dashboard of sorts.

I have done this with Huddles I have led, and it has proven to be an effective way of synthesizing all that we have talked about in this book when it comes to awakening discipleship and mission among those to whom we speak. So I offer this dashboard to you as a tool that can help you design and evaluate your communication.

COMMUNICATION DASHBOARD

CONTENT	CONTEXT	CONVERSION
Message	History	Calling
Metanarrative	Biography	Challenge
Meme	Stance	Completion
REVELATION	RELATIONSHIP	RESPONSE

CONTENT

Content is the section in which we talk about Message, Metanarrative, and Meme. This is what we excavate from the landscape of life.

MESSAGE
- What is the message that God has given me for this audience at this time?
- How does it connect to my personal perspective on the Gospel and to the Biblical gospel as a whole?

METANARRATIVE
- Which themes in your message can you find in different sections of Scripture?
- Are there specific biblical heroes who exemplify these things?
- How can you refer to this metanarrative easily in your communication?

MEME
- What memes can you use to communicate your message?
- Are they simple, transferrable, and repeatable? Give examples of each trait.
- Do they other a picture of God, a mirror on ourselves, and a window on the world? Give examples of each of these.
- Do they have adaptability, longevity, and fecundity? Give examples.
- Is the content solid? Is the form understandable? Is the stance helpful? Give examples of each of these traits.

CONTEXT

Context is the area where we talk about History, Biography, and Stance and make connections between them.

HISTORY

- What is the history of the context where you are communicating?
- What are the connections between the history of your context and the themes of your message? (For example, themes of virtues or vices in the history of your context.)

BIOGRAPHY

- What is the biography of the people to whom you are communicating?
- Are there specific testimonies or stories from the biography of your audience that it would be appropriate to use in your communication? If so, what are they, and how can you use them?

STANCE

- What are the cultural texts of your context? What stance should you take toward each of them?
- What are the linguistic codes in your context? What stance should you take toward them?
- What are the other voices in your context? What stance should you take toward them?
- Who is your audience? What stance do you need to take specifically about them?

CONVERSION

The conversion step where we highlight the hero's journey and use it to lead our audience through the Call, the Challenge, and the Completion of the journey.

CALL

- How will your communication call your audience into the hero's journey?
- How will your communication help your audience hear and answer the specific call God is placing on their lives?
- In what ways will your audience be most tempted to reject the call? How can you help them overcome this tendency?

CHALLENGE

- How can you honestly illustrate the challenge of the valley along the journey? Why is it important for you to do this?
- How can you encourage the heroes in your audience to keep traveling and keep excavating in the valley of the desert?
- How can your communication help people see and listen to the mentors and friends around them?

COMPLETION

- How will your communication paint a picture of the completion of the journey and the blessings found there?
- How will you encourage people to embark on new journeys as heroes? How will you encourage them to use their bounties to serve as friends and mentors for others?

THE FULL ARC

If you review this dashboard as you complete your preparation for a speaking event, a sermon series, a retreat or conference, or some other kind of speaking event or communication venue, you will get a wide-angle view of what else you need to consider to be the kind of communicator that awakens his or her audience. One big-picture way to evaluate your communication is whether it moves in the direction of:

- Revelation: Does it reveal God and what he is doing in the world?
- Relationship: Does it connect to the audience in a meaningful way?
- Response: Does it help the audience respond with a tangible next step?

If your communication takes this shape, you will see God using it as part of his awakening work in your context. So use this dashboard as you fulfill your calling as a communicator, and as you seek to awaken the heroes in your context to find their own gospels and embark on their own journeys.

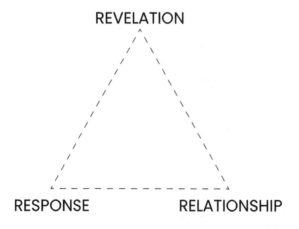

REVELATION

RESPONSE   RELATIONSHIP

USING THE TRIANGLE TO UNDERSTAND SPEAK OUT

Throughout my ministry, I have used shapes as memes to transfer simple, repeatable concepts of discipleship to people I disciple and to larger congregations and groups. So it will come as no surprise that, as I began to develop the ideas found in this book, I pictured them as three triangles within a larger triangle.

Ultimately, I decided it was also helpful to use additional shapes—the *Landscape of Life* for content, the *Connected Nexus* for context, and *The Hero's Journey* for conversion. These are the shapes used throughout the book.

But if you're used to using triangles to understand concepts— as many in the larger 3DM movement are—then I thought it might be helpful to depict the big ideas covered in *Speak Out* on a triangle. Feel free to use either set of shapes or both as you consider, practice, and share these ideas.

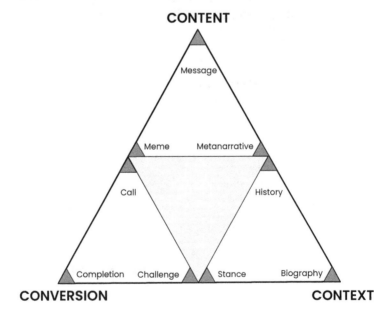

CONCLUSION

The man and woman are waiting outside the airport in a mist that is typical of London weather.

They are tired with red eyes after a long flight. They signal for the next Uber in line and load the bags into the trunk while the Uber driver turns around and asks directions. The driver has a full head of dark, curly hair clipped close to his head, which shows his youthful dark face. He is wearing two sweaters and a scarf inside the car.

The man immediately begins to talk and ask a couple of questions, which confirms what he first thought. The young driver is from Ethiopia, having arrived in the U.K. just a few years earlier, and having never grown accustomed to the cold.

The man in the back of the car is his opposite in every way — an older, white-haired gentleman with a strong English accent despite being recently sworn in as an American citizen.

To anyone outside this car, these two men would seem to have little to connect them, but their conversation began to unfold as the London landscape passed by.

The man in the back seat recognizes this young man's heritage and knew the country's political and spiritual history. He shares some of these insights, and the driver responds, at first surprised but then becomes more animated and warm.

By the end of the short, 20-minute drive, the older man is sharing some of his gospel and some of the gospel, giving hope to the driver. He is putting into practice unconsciously what he has written in this book.

Each principle that has been outlined in the previous chapters can bring about an awakening either in a large group or in this man's case, to an individual Uber driver. What is required is that we speak out and let this process begin.

I wrote this book in Greenville, South Carolina. I moved there a few years ago for a time of pruning and abiding. During this time, I focused on communication and awakening—the content you find in this book—through academic study, and through pilot Huddles that have helped to test and refine these ideas. I've started to travel and speak to introduce these ideas to church leaders around the world. And as I have travelled this journey of excavation, God has revealed the next leg of my hero's journey as a preaching team lead at Apex Church in the Dayton, Ohio, area.

I believe all this is important. In fact, I believe that these ideas have the potential to be as helpful to people as the ideas in *Building a Discipling Culture* have been over the last 10 years.

During our time in Greenville, I have been huddling leaders around the country through videoconferences. I basically have spent all day Tuesday, Wednesday, and Thursday discipling leaders. Sally has been huddling women on family on mission.

We have also reached out into my new context to find People of Peace. We started in my neighborhood slowly, and after about a year we started to see a real sense of family emerge. Every Monday evening, we had a group of this family in our home for our weekly "Made it through Monday" meal. Since our move to Dayton, we hope and pray they have continued.

Those of us who are following Jesus' command to make disciples need to understand how to awaken people to the hero's journey God sets before them, to listen to the Holy Spirit, and to follow Jesus' example. We need to live real life with people in a family context, discovering the mission God wants us to go on together.

I'm thankful that God has helped me understand more fully over the past few years how awakening, discipleship, and mission work together in an intentional and not just an intuitive way. I pray expectantly for everyone who reads this book — whether a pastor, a teacher, or a lay person — that God will use them to speak out and spark an awakening of discipleship and mission wherever their context may be.

―――――――――――――

At the beginning of *Speak Out*, I suggested that there was a journey that you and I would be going on together: from content to context to conversion; from revelation to relationship and through to response.

I hope by now you can see while we have been on this journey, we have sought to stay in step with the Holy Spirit as He has trained us in the skills of the New Testament preachers. I believe now you are ready and prepared to go and try to speak out and step into a world of gospel communication.

APPENDIX A

MAKING DISCIPLES THROUGH MISSIONAL PREACHING

Author's note: This appendix is adapted from a chapter I wrote for *Missional Disciple-Making: Disciple-Making for the Purpose of Mission*, edited by David M. Gustafson, Ph.D., and myself.[1] Available at 3dmpublishing.com, *Missional Disciple-Making* is a collection of essays by missional scholars and scholarly practitioners who have thought deeply, critically, and analytically about making disciples in a context of mission for the purpose of mission.

This book is an attempt to offer a scholarly examination of missional discipleship. As contributors we have come to the subject both as disciples seeking to embrace the call to make disciples and as missiologists seeking to understand the means by which discipleship might take place through the ecclesia of Jesus Christ. Missiology is by its very nature multi–disciplinary, and so we have brought a variety of academic disciplines to bear upon the subject.

---

1   Michael Breen, "Making Disciples through Missional Preaching," *Missional Disciple-Making: Disciple-making for the purpose of mission*," ed. Michael J. Breen and David M. Gustafson (3DM Publishing, 2019), 253-279.

In keeping with this multi-disciplinary missiological perspective, I will be leaning on a variety of scholarly disciplines as I attempt to explore the catalytic effects of preaching on the disciple-making process. Unfortunately I will not be able to draw on a large missiological corpus on the subject[2] because, although there is a large body of theological scholarship covering the subjects of homiletics and its various connections to oration and the growing world of communication studies and sociolinguistics, the preaching event as an expression of the Mission of God is barely addressed in missiological scholarship.[3]

This paucity is particularly surprising when we consider that the vast majority of Christian sermons are drawn directly from Scripture—the foundational theological text of missiology— and that the context of preaching is most often the ecclesia of Jesus Christ—the principle instrument of Missio Dei. Listening to a sermon is the single event that connects more Christians across the world and through the centuries than any other corporate event. The Eucharist—which across the various traditions of Christianity is celebrated universally—is encountered far less than the sermon. In fact, we could say that the delivery and reception of a sermon is the ubiquitous experience of Christian worship.

Although I'm sure we might be able to find a number of legitimate explanations for this lacuna, the task of finding them lies well beyond the scope of this chapter. Here I hope to address a simpler and singularly more edifying question: How can the preaching event be catalytic of the disciple-making process? In answer I propose to offer two particular pathways in which we can begin to explore this vital relationship.

The first pathway I wish to explore is *contextualization*; the process by which we connect our lives and the message of the gospel we hope to convey within the preaching event to those

---

2   Trinity Journal Vol. 33, No. 2, 2012 is a notable attempt at addressing this issue.

3   An exception is Rochelle Cathcart's excellent "Preaching and Culture: An In-Depth Analysis of the Engagement with Culture in the Sermons of Rob Bell, Timothy Keller and Michael Pfleger." Deerfield, Illinois, December 2011.

among whom we live, and thus by which we partner with God in communicating the Good News of salvation to the world.

The second pathway is *mimesis*; the process of imitation— always at the heart of any thoroughgoing approach to discipleship—in which we join Jesus in his work of making disciples.

Contextualization helps preachers connect with potential disciples in their audience.

Mimesis helps them offer exemplars of the teaching offered so the contextualized message can be lived out and applied by their audience.

It is my contention that if we are to create spiritual ecosystems in which discipleship naturally emerges—ecclesial cultures from which relationships with pre-Christians naturally develop and in which the imitation of the life of Jesus Christ is the normative expression of the life of a Christian believer—we will need to deepen our understanding of the skills of both contextualization and mimesis.

CONTEXTUALIZATION

On the feast of John the Baptist (June 24) in 401 A.D., St. Augustine preached a seminal message on John 1. Preaching in Latin to a cosmopolitan congregation in the North African city of Hippo, Augustine spoke about Vox and Verbum[4]. There is a Voice (Vox) and there is the Word (Verbum). John the Baptist is the "voice crying in the wilderness" (John 1:23, c.f. Is. 40:3), and Jesus Christ is "the Word made flesh" (John 1:14). It appears that Augustine hoped to impress upon his congregation that the Word (Verbum)—the second person of the Trinity, the Son of God made flesh in the person of Jesus Christ of Nazareth—is always prior to the Voice (Vox), whether

---

4   For an interesting discussion on the influence of Augustine on European language with references to this sermon, see Vivian Law's *The History of Linguistics in Europe from Plato to 1600*, University of Cambridge, 2003.

that be the noble voice of the Baptizer, Augustine's own, or that of the individuals in his audience.

Augustine encouraged his audience to consider that Jesus the Word is always present within them, whether their capacity to be a Voice was active or not. Perhaps reflecting his Neo-platonic leanings, he suggested that the Word is always resident within the believing person and is revealed as it is "translated" into the language of the audience to which it is addressed. He illustrated this by describing himself walking through the marketplace in Hippo. The Word within him, resident in the person of Jesus Christ, could be translated into Latin, Greek, or even Punic (the language of ancient Carthage) before it was communicated through him to those around him in the marketplace.

If we are to follow the Bishop of Hippo's argument, we have to conclude that we have the same role as Augustine himself, to be translator and as such contextualizer of the divine revelation of the Holy Trinity resident within us as the Word (or Verbum). Contextualized communication is something that begins as an impulse within the individual Christian—in response to the presence of the missionary God resident within us. According to Augustine this occurs first by him conveying the revelation of his presence *within us*, and second by conveying that same revelation *through us*. It is God, committed as he is to incarnate revelation, who seeks to reveal himself in our lives and through our lives—through our thoughts, words, and actions. By this we become the conduits of the contextualized Gospel to the world.

These seminal ideas on contextualization taught by Augustine have influenced discussion within the world of linguistics and translation studies to this day. Professor Andrew Walls, writing on the history of translation and reflecting on the same scriptural passage as Augustine, comes to some very similar conclusions; for him too the first example of contextual translation is that which occurred when God the Word became flesh and dwelt among us (John 1:14).[5]

Andrew Chesterman indicates something of the debate that surrounds the disciplines of contextualized translation when he highlights the need for sensitivity when considering the target audience. In his fascinating book *Memes of Translation*, he reflects on the early ideas of "Logos" or "Word" that reflect the intellectual milieu of Augustine and then draws a distinction between a "free" and "literal" translation. In a way Augustine, by his use of Vox and Verbum, is suggesting that all of our attempts to convey the Word of God to others is a "free translation". But being a "free translation" does not mean that the communication of God's Word is less faithful than a 'literal translation"; in fact it may mean that there is simply an increased sensitivity to the context in which we are communicating. To some extent all human articulations of the divine Word are dependent on a negotiation between human freedom and divine sovereignty, and on the relationship between human sinfulness and a perfect God resident within us.[6]

This Augustinian distinction between Christ resident within the believer and them as mediators of his revelation requires that we come to an understanding of the role of the Holy Scriptures.

Those like me who find the Written Word to be of central significance in Christian discipleship will of course apply this Augustinian proposition by suggesting that any "internal" revelation of God received through the mediation of the presence the Word of God within us be brought to the bar of Scripture so that our internal promptings can be understood and codified by the definitive revelation we find in the Bible. The living Word—Jesus Christ—resident within us by his Spirit is understood most clearly as we reflect on the Written Word.

5   Andrew Walls, "The Translation Principle in Christian History" (p.25) in *Studies in Christian Mission*, Ed. Peggy Brock, James Grayson, and David Maxwell, 1990.

6   Andrew Chesterman, *Memes of Translation: The spread of ideas in translation theory*, John Benjamins, 2016, 24.

And so we hold the Holy Scriptures like a mirrored lens to clarify and focus what it is that we sense God is saying to us and through us. More of this later.

Recently the world of neuroscience has advanced some suggestions as to why Augustine's ideas presented in his sermon on Vox and Verbum are so important to the discussion of contextualization. In his fascinating and erudite book *The Master and his Emissary*, Ian McGilchrist goes beyond the "pop" science understanding of the bi-hemispherical life of the brain, familiar to many, and describes the foundational and necessary process that links the two hemispheres together.[7] Revealing how the left hemisphere's capacity for category and vocabulary when connected to the right hemisphere's ability for context and mystery provide the broader vision and understanding of the world that we need for survival and success, McGilchrist makes a compelling case for always striving to combine both the large encompassing perspective of the right hemisphere with the smaller more categorical perspective of the left. Only when we hold together both views do we have the "necessary distance" to grasp a comprehensive understanding of our world. Such a perspective offers a far more complete interpretation of our experience. It is here, in the interplay between the left and right hemispheres, that the internal process of translation to which Augustine refers—and which is the first and essential stage of contextualization—takes place.

One of McGilchrist's principal concerns is to demonstrate that our perception of the world is no longer defined by a reflexive relationship between the two hemispheres but is now dominated by the empiricism and categorization of the left hemisphere. To illustrate he uses what appears to be an ancient tale told about a king and his vizier; our world is captive to the scientific and empirical perspective of "the emissary" and devoid of the spiritual and mystical perspective of "the master". The right hemisphere—offering the wisdom

---

7   Ian McGilchrist. (2009). *The Master and his Emissary: The divided brain and the making of the Western world*, London, Yale University Press, 2009. I cite the Amazon Kindle version through this chapter.

of contextualization—has been usurped by the vizier—the left hemisphere—offering only syntax, data and category. We are "ruled" by "the emissary" rather than "the master:,

> At present the domain—our civilization—finds itself in the hands of the vizier, who, however gifted, is effectively an ambitious regional bureaucrat with his own interests at heart. Meanwhile the master, the one whose wisdom gave the people peace and security, is led away in chains. The master is betrayed by his emissary.[8]

If McGilchrist is right, and the vast weight of evidence amassed in his neuroscientific research appears to suggest that he is, the task of translating and communicating the Word of God, resident within us in the person of Jesus Christ, can only be successfully accomplished if we embrace the skill sets associated with both aspects of our mental life—those that are represented by the left hemisphere and those that are represented by the right hemisphere of the brain. The task of contextualization will always rely on our commitment to engage the dialectic interplay between the content of divine revelation—the Word of God—and the context, found in the world that God has made and in which we live. If we follow McGilchrist's argument, our own inner workings—found in the interconnection of our bi-hemispherical brain—must be taken seriously as the nexus of our initial attempts at contextualization. What happens within us must first be considered before we ever try to express what is happening without. The reflexive connection between the content and context of divine revelation (whether the context be our internal or external world) creates a binocular vision of the world providing us with depth in our field of perception.

This approach, that emphasizes the need for the large (right hemisphere—contextualizing) and small (left hemisphere—content-clarifying) pictures of the world, resonates deeply with the work of other theologians and thinkers from quite different

---

8   Ibid., loc493 (Kindle)

fields of scholarship. Perhaps in this we find the suggestion of a key concept that helps us understand the epistemological basis for a variety of scholarly perspectives. Allow me to suggest two, one from the world of biblical theology and the other from sociology.

Anthony Thistleton's "Two Horizons" approach to biblical interpretation is an excellent example for what McGilchrist is arguing.[9] As one of the most respected evangelical biblical theologians of recent years, Thistleton suggests that the hermeneutical process requires we take account of both the first horizon of the biblical milieu and the second horizon of the world in which we live. We should examine how the Word of God in Scripture was embraced and used by its original recipients and also how it appears to function in our own society and culture. He persuasively contends that, by holding these two horizons together, we arrive at a usable meaning of the text. Though Thiselton's hermeneutical model identifies somewhat different categories of observation, it still requires we hold together both the large and the small perceptive field; the large picture of the metanarrative of Scripture interacting with the variety of human cultures from which it emerged, alongside the smaller picture of our own social and cultural setting in which God's Word is currently operative. We need both hemispheres of the brain to understand both scriptural horizons. But the reflexive process at the heart of human mental activity seems to establish the basis for Thiselton's hermeneutic.

Of course we need both hemispheres of the brain to grasp Thiselton's two horizons, but it is the reflexive interplay between the hemispheres that appears to establish the pattern of thought that underlies Thiselton's approach. In fact if we were to bring together the insights of Augustine and Thiselton, a pattern appears to emerge that suggests a continuous

---

9   A.C. Thiselton, *The Two Horizons: New Testament Hermeneutics and Philosophical Description with Special Reference to Heidegger, Bultmann, Gadamer, and Wittgenstein,* Carlisle, U, The Paternoster Press, 1980.

reflexive interplay—something that looks like a continuous spiraling process of reflection.[10]

For Augustine the interpretive process begins in the "inner life" of each Christian as we seek to receive and understand the Word of God for ourselves. The process continues to inevitably include other people as we attempt to translate and communicate the content of this divine revelation with those in our social and cultural setting. For Thiselton the smaller context is not an internal mental state but rather that of our social and cultural context, and the larger is the historical, social, and cultural setting of the bible. Both Augustine and Thiselton describe a binocular vision derived from combining both the larger and smaller perspective. The interaction between the hemispheres of the brain may be said to provide a template or perhaps an analogue of the epistemology of both Augustine and Thiselton.

It is important to stress that I and more importantly neuroscientists like McGilchrist are not suggesting that there is a necessary relationship between one hemisphere of the brain and one of Thiselton's horizons or one part of Augustine's internal revelatory processes. We clearly need both hemispheres for an adequate perception of the world. But perhaps we can suggest that the interplay between the hemispheres does provide a pattern of perception that emerges in a variety of scholarly views. Could it be that these two theologians, separated by so many centuries, are describing the same reflective process spiraling from the internal perceptions of an individual Christian through the immediate social and cultural context to the broader context of the biblical narrative and back again? Augustine reveals the process occurring in the "heart"—the inner life—of the believer; the other, that of Thistleton, reveals what is occurring in the interplay between the historical context of the Bible and that of our own day.

---

10   Though beyond the remit of this study an apparent elucidation on the epistemological implications of this idea can be found in Hofstadter's classic publication *Gödel, Escher, Bach: An Eternal Golden Braid*, Basic Books, 1979.

Bringing these insights together enables us to understand how the internal witness to the presence of God within the believer can be brought to the bar of Scripture. In this we begin to see how the living Word—Jesus Christ—living within us by his Spirit witnesses to and confirms his written Word. When we set this inner reflexive process against what we see of the use of the scriptures in their own social and cultural settings, we begin to visualize the possibility of thoroughgoing contextualizing hermeneutic, one that is fully operative in our daily lives. Surely it is this kind of clarity and confidence in the process of God's self-revealing work that equips us for a convincing presentation of the Gospel to the audience of our missional context.

To me this is hugely significant; in fact, I would go so far as to say that this reflexive process, starting in the inner life of every believer and spiraling through time and place, is at the heart of all genuine contextualization of the gospel. It is the binocular vision, derived via the interplay of the larger (historical, social, cultural) and smaller (personal, familial, ecclesial) context that gives us what we might call a three-dimensional view of context.

If in our formal and informal proclamation of the gospel we used this methodology, we would present to the current and potential disciples of Jesus Christ a model that they could readily replicate and multiply. If preachers and teachers would teach and preach in this way to the gathered company of the ecclesia, surely the church would be more ably equipped to reach out to the variety of social settings of our mission to the world.

A fuller understanding of the potential for a replicative process would require an understanding of how imitation takes place as the Word of God is proclaimed, and to this I will attend a little later in the chapter, but first, to complete our discussion of the subject of contextualization, I would like to offer one final example that speaks directly to our examination of missional preaching.

In the mid-20th century, C. Wright Mills described sociology as a subject blighted by the battle between the proponents of what he called the sociology of the Grand Theory and that of Abstract Empiricism. One set of sociologists were always working from the perspective of the great systems and structures that undergird our culture, while the others described our social settings purely in terms of the empirical data derived from them.

In a stroke of genius Mills brought the benefits of both approaches together in a single idea, something he called "The Sociological Imagination"—an idea that influences prominent sociologists even to this day.[11] With this he was able to hold together both the *history* of the social and cultural context and the *biography* of those living within it. As he says,

> We have come to know that every individual lives, from one generation to the next, in some society; that he lives out a biography and that he lives it out within some historical sequence. By the fact of his living he contributes, however minutely, to the shaping of this society and to the course of its history, even as he is made by society and by its historical push and shove.

> The sociological imagination enables us to grasp history and biography and the relations between the two within society. That is its task and its promise. To recognize this task and this promise is the mark of the classic social analyst.'[12]

Arguing for the use of this kind of thinking among the influencers, academics, and public intellectuals, he describes the sociological imagination as,

---

11   Christian Smith with Melinda Lundquist Denton, *Soul Searching: The Religious and Spiritual Lives of American Teenagers*, Oxford University Press, 2005, p. 763.

12   C. Wright Mills, *The Sociological Imagination*, New York, Oxford University Press, 2000, p. 24 (ibooks).

> (A) quality of mind that will help them use information
> and to develop a reason in order to achieve lucid
> summations of what is going on in the world and of what
> may be happening within themselves. It is this quality,
> I'm going to contend, the journalists and scholars, artists
> and publics, scientists and editors are coming to expect
> of what may be called the sociological imagination.[13]

Mills appears to be describing the very same process of
reflection that we see in the work of Augustine and Thiselton
and to which McGilchrist points. The "lucid summations" to
which Mills refers are, I think, what I mean when I speak of an
in-depth binocular vision.

Interestingly Mills goes on to describe, in near revelatory
language, what happens when we bring the small and large
picture together.

> The sociological imagination is the most fruitful form
> of this self-consciousness. By its use men whose
> mentalities have swept only a series of limited orbits
> often come to *feel as if suddenly awakened* in the house
> with which they had only supposed themselves to be
> familiar. Correctly or incorrectly, they often come to feel
> that they can now provide themselves with adequate
> summations, cohesive assessments, comprehensive
> orientations.[14] (emphasis mine)

This begins to suggest that clarity of understanding –in a
number of areas of human intellectual endeavor—is only found
when we take on the task of binocular vision—holding together
the small and the large pictures of our reflective engagement.

Now it is possible to connect all that we have been considering
on the subject of contextualization. The two hemispheres of
the brain provide us with the necessary template of a binocular

---

13   Ibid., p.21 (ibooks).

14   Ibid., p.29 (ibooks).

vision of the small and large perspectives; this mental activity appears to be reflected and articulated in the epistemologies of each of these scholars.

It would appear that the neural process catalyzes a binocular vision of the world spiraling from the inner life of each individual believer through the written Word of God—itself the product of the same kind of process—into our local social and cultural context and into the sweeping arc of history out of which our culture has emerged. Preachers who successfully contextualize the gospel to their missional setting begin by first hearing the Living Word within them. By applying this internal revelation—through the filter of the Written Word—to their own lives, these preachers embrace a process that spirals out in ever-widening circles from their own inner life into their surrounding world and back again to their own inner world. It is this spiraling process that results in a thoroughgoing approach to contextualization.

Acts 2:14-41: Then Peter stood up with the Eleven, raised his voice and addressed the crowd: "Fellow Jews and all of you who live in Jerusalem, let me explain this to you; listen carefully to what I say. These men are not drunk, as you suppose. It's only nine in the morning!"

Biography: Peter immediately connects with the crowd that has gathered because of the spectacular events surrounding the outpouring of the Holy Spirit on the day of Pentecost. He connects himself and the 120 disciples with the crowd, suggesting that they share the same cultural expectations—that no one would be drunk at 9 o'clock in the morning.

*No, this is what was spoken
by the prophet Joel:*
'In the last days, God says,
  I will pour out my Spirit on
  all people.
Your sons and daughters
  will prophesy,
  your young men will see
  visions,
your old men will dream
  dreams.
Even on my servants, both
  men and women,

I will pour out my Spirit in
  those days,
  and they will prophesy.
I will show wonders in the
  heaven above
  and signs on the earth
  below,
  blood and fire and billows
  of smoke.
The sun will be turned to
  darkness and the moon to
  blood
before the coming of the
  great and glorious day of
  the Lord.
And everyone who calls on
  the name of the Lord will be
  saved.

History: Peter connects the experience of the disciples and the crowd with the big picture of biblical prophecy and messianic expectation. Many scholars believe that eschatological expectations at out almost fever pitch during the days of Jesus and the early apostles. Here Peter is connecting with prophetic material that many of his audience might have been familiar during this period in Israel's history.

"Men of Israel, listen to this: Jesus of Nazareth was a man accredited by God to you by miracles, wonders and signs, which God did among you through him, as you yourselves know. This man was handed over to you by God's set purpose and foreknowledge; and you, with the help of wicked men, put him to death by nailing him to the cross. But God raised him from the dead, freeing him from the agony of death, because it was impossible for death to keep its hold on him." "Men of Israel, listen to this: Jesus of Nazareth was a man accredited by God to you by miracles, wonders and signs, which God did among you through him, as you yourselves know. This man was handed over to you by God's set purpose and foreknowledge; and you, with the help of wicked men, put him to death by nailing him to the cross. But God raised him from the dead, freeing him from the agony of death, because it was impossible for death to keep its hold on him."

Biography: Peter moves from the broader picture of the biblical metanarrative and again draws the attention of his audience to their own biographies and their experience in recent days. They all are witnesses to the events that have taken place in Jerusalem.

Let us look to Scripture for an example of how this may happen. In Peter's sermon on the day of Pentecost, we see how assuming a binocular vision in preaching helps to contextualize a preached message to the audience. Peter alternates between inner world and outer world – or to put it another way, between history and biography – to bring the small picture and big picture together in an understandable yet memorable manner. The following excerpts show how Peter did this.

Contextualization is key to disciple-making.

But of course any gospel message, however well contextualized, requires a means by which the audience is able to apply the message to their own lives. In consideration of this, we will need to venture into the somewhat troubled academic waters of mimesis.

MIMESIS

Imitation has always been foundational to the understanding of what it means to be a disciple Jesus Christ. Imitating the conduct of great religious leaders was something well known both in contemporary Judaism and in the broader Greco-Roman world of the mystery religions in the New Testament period. Imitation—becoming what your leader is rather than just learning what your leader knows—was foundational to anyone considering the cost of discipleship. [15]

This is clearly articulated in the Johannine record of the words of Jesus

> Believe me when I say that I am in the Father and the
> Father is in me; or at least believe on the evidence of
> the miracles themselves. I tell you the truth; anyone who
> has faith in me *will do what I have been doing*. He will do

---

15   Michael Wilkins develops this point in one of the few scholarly treatments
     of the subject of discipleship, *Following the Master: A Biblical Theology of
     Discipleship*, Zondervan, 1992, p. 63ff.

even greater things than these, because I am going to
the Father. (John 14:11-12 italics mine)

Clearly Jesus expected his disciples to imitate his conduct.

Likewise, it appears that the Pauline Church also expected
those who were being nurtured in the Christian faith engage in
imitation,

> You became imitators of us and of the Lord; in spite
> of severe suffering, you welcomed the message with
> the joy given by the Holy Spirit. And so you became a
> model to all the believers in Macedonia and Achaia. The
> Lord's message rang out from you not only in Macedonia
> and Achaia–your faith in God has become known
> everywhere. (1 Thess.1: 6-8)

For the Thessalonians the imitation process was reproductive.
First they imitated Paul, and then others imitated them. This
imitative process became an authenticating mark of the gospel
they proclaimed. The same can be said of the Christians
addressed in the Corinthian correspondence,

> Therefore I urge you to imitate me. For this reason, I
> am sending to you Timothy, my son whom I love, who is
> faithful in the Lord. He will remind you of my way of life in
> Christ Jesus, which agrees with what I teach everywhere
> in every church. (1 Cor. 4:16-17)

Again the injunction is to imitate—on this occasion a mimetic
exemplar—someone who represented the pattern of imitation
in their own life. Paul believes that Timothy has effectively
imitated his life and so now can be trusted as a mimetic
exemplar and as such an apostolic representative. Again the
mimetic process authenticates the message proclaimed.

Offering such an encouragement to mimesis in our
communication of the Gospel will allow our audience to

engage at a visceral level with our message. Writing from a
neuroscientific point of view, McGilchrist says,

> The enormous strength of the human capacity for
> mimesis is that our brains let us escape from the
> confines of our own experience and enter directly into
> the experience of another being: this is the way in which,
> through human consciousness, we bridge the gap, share
> in what another feels and does, in what it is like to be
> that person. This comes about through our ability to
> transform what we perceive into something we directly
> experience.[16]

Having followed other arguments offered by McGilchrist, we
would naturally expect that his empirical observations lead us
to an understanding that mimesis requires the engagements
of both the left and the right hemispheres of the brain—
particularly the right side—and such is the case.

> As might be expected, there is significantly increased
> right-sided activity in the limbic system specifically
> during imitation, compared with mere observation,
> of emotional facial expressions. There is even some
> evidence that we identify objectively with people with
> whom we share a common purpose—when we are
> co-operating in a task, for example—to such a degree
> that we seem to merge identity with them. In ingeniously
> designed experiments where two participants are sitting
> next to one another, sharing a combined task, but with
> functionally independent roles, the two individuals
> appear spontaneously to function as one agent with a
> unified action plan.[17]

---

16   McGilchrist, loc. 6504 (Kindle)

17   Ibid., loc. 6519 (Kindle)

Mimesis therefore is at the very heart of what it means to be a learning human being—from the beginning of life imitation is what makes us who we are,

Imitation is non-instrumental. It is intrinsically pleasurable, and babies and small children indulge in it for its own sake. The process is fundamental and hard-wired, and babies as little as forty-five minutes old can imitate facial gestures. It is how we get to know what we know, but also how we become who we are.[18]

If this is true of what it means to be human, then surely this mimetic process lies at the heart of the discipling process. The person being discipled clearly is able to "share in what another feels and does, in what it is like to be that person"[19]— especially when the other person is his or her discipler, attempting to pass on what he or she has experienced as he or she has followed Christ. The disciple shares in what it is like for the discipler to imitate Christ, or perhaps what it is like to emulate the lives of other mimetic exemplars that the discipler considers worthy of consideration. Therefore, the discipling process—which probably always involves imitation to some extent—gives access to our ability to "transform that which we perceive into something we directly experience".[20]

Clearly if preaching is to help the ecclesia of Jesus Christ to be formed in his image, imitative patterns and mimetic exemplars (drawn from the worlds of the Bible, history and our contemporary and personal lives) will need to be prominently present in our proclamation. Fortunately, mimesis is hardwired by our Creator into the very fabric of our lives. And so developing patterns of imitative thought and conduct in our preaching should not be beyond any of us.

---

18   Ibid., loc. 6531 (Kindle)

19   See page 222.

20   See page 222.

MIMESIS AND MEMES

Of course this discussion on mimesis thrusts us directly into the fraught and hotly contested landscape of mimetics and the idea that cultural evolution takes place via the transfer of packets of cultural information—memes—passed from one person to another. And this in turn forces us to consider whether memes, if they exist, behave—as some have suggested—like their genetic counterparts, and develop semiautonomous lives of their own, adapting, reproducing, and assimilating into their hosts.

It would be fair to say that a study of memes lies on the boundaries of what would normally be expected from our particular area of missiological concern. But given that any examination of the mission of God inevitably draws us to a consideration of the Great Commission, it should not surprise us that this in turn leads us to a consideration of discipleship and imitation and from there to a consideration of memes.

In 1976 Richard Dawkins—now famous for his aggressive form of proselytizing atheism—was seeking to summarize the state of play in his own scholarly field of genetics. *The Selfish Gene* was an overnight international success. Toward the end of the book Dawkins, attempting to identify and explain the difference between humans and all other species suggested that culture—in the mind of Dawkins a distinctly human creation—is generated through the transfer of memes. For Dawkins memes, like genes, are replicators that establish a competitive advantage within the broader meme pool through adaptability, fecundity, and longevity. For Dawkins such memes as "God", "hellfire", and "celibacy" are best explained through the transmission of a meme contagion from one brain to another. For him memes are how human beings have communicated cultural information to one another since the beginnings of our species. He contends that because of our highly evolved mental capacity, we unlike other meme bearing species have the ability to assert some control over the process,

> We are built as gene machines and cultured as meme
> machines, but we have the power to turn against our
> creators, we, alone on earth can rebel against the
> tyranny of the selfish replicator. [21]

Since the publication of this seminal work, mimetics has
taken two quite different directions; some like Dawkins have
focused on describing and discovering memes functioning in
the brain—these are the mentalists. Biological anthropologist
Robert Aunger[22] would perhaps be the best-known example of
a scholar in this camp; he along with Susan Blackmore[23] has
led the way in defining memes as contagions transmitted from
one brain to another. Here the meme and the meme host have
a separate existence. Others, describing the emergence of
culture through behaviors and artifacts, have been positioned
as behaviorists, with Derek Gatherer[24] perhaps the most
influential. In this approach the meme and the meme vehicle
are inseparable—the meme has no independent existence
outside of the behavior that supports it.

In some ways the central ground between these two
increasingly hardening contra positions is found in the
use of the memes and mimesis in *neuroscience*—where
neuroscientists are able to observe changes in the brain
through neuroimaging techniques as people learn—and
communication studies and sociolinguistics—especially where
research has focused on the use and spread of Internet
memes.

As we observed earlier, neuroscientists are now able to
observe the intra-cranial activity that occurs during imitation
and have provided some helpful insights into an understanding
of the imitation process. In a short paper "Mirror Neurons

21   Richard Dawkins, *The Selfish Gene*, Oxford University Press, 1989, p. 201

22   Robert Aunger, *The Electric Meme*, Simon & Schuster, 2002.

23   Susan Blackmore, *The Meme Machine*, Oxford University Press, 1999.

24   Derek Gatherer, "Why the 'Thought Contagion' Metaphor is Retarding the
     Progress of Memetics," School of Biomolecular Sciences Liverpool, John
     Moores University, 1998.

and Imitation Learning as the Driving Force behind 'The Great Leap Forward' in Human Evolution"[25], the distinguished neuroscientist V.S. Ramachandran details the discovery of neurons that appear to be specifically adapted to activate during human imitation. As the name suggests, mirror neurons appear to allow participants in a learning process to mirror the behavior of others. First identified in the brains of monkeys, these "mirror neurons" help us mimic behavior from one person to another. When we take this along with the evidence offered by McGilchrist for a behavioral understanding of imitation, it would appear that memes—particularly those described by Dawkins—are not necessary for a thorough description of human imitation.

Such a conclusion appears to be equally true when we consider memes from the point of view of communication studies and sociolinguistics.

Limor Shifman of the Hebrew University, Jerusalem—whose work on Internet memes is definitive in the field—posits that the vernacular use of the term "meme" across the Internet does not require an acceptance of Dawkins' definition. Rather, Shifman suggests that Internet memes are combinations of cultural symbols circulated, imitated, and transformed by individual users, creating a shared cultural experience. These are not in her opinion single ideas or formulas propagating from brain to brain and manifesting in the medium of cyberspace. As she says,

> First, memes may best be understood as pieces of *cultural information that pass along from person to person, but gradually scale into a shared social phenomenon.* Although they spread on a micro basis, their impact is on the macro level: memes shape the mindsets, forms of behavior, and actions of social groups. This attribute is highly compatible to the way culture is formed in the Web 2.0 era, which is marked by

---

25   V.S. Ramachandran, "Mirror Neurons and Imitation Learning as the Driving Force Behind the Great Leap Forward in Human Evolution," From the Third Culture, http://www.edge.org/3rd_culture/

platforms for creating and exchanging user-generated content.[26]

This description suggests that Internet memes are products of contemporary culture—artifacts of the newly created social context of cyberspace—rather than creators of it. As such Shifman's approach is similar to the position reached a decade earlier by the cognitive anthropologist Scott Atran.[27]

For Shifman, Internet memes bear a close resemblance to the processes identified within diffusion studies and as such[28], even though they are not what some mimeticists might hope them to be, can be observed and measured. And although the exact contribution to the development of human culture maybe questioned, Internet memes are definitely doing something. When commenting on the catalytic processes that occur in the transmission and multiplication of YouTube memes, Shifman says,

> It is the proposition that what is actually being replicated on YouTube is the practice of creating simple and repetitive content traits identified here as catalysts for imitation by others. Transplanting this to the realm of ideas would suggest that more than anything, these memetic videos spread the notion of participatory culture itself: a culture based on the active spread and re-creation of content by users.[29]

For Shifman Internet Memes have three vital components— *content, form and stance.* Of these three distinct components, *stance*, built on the earlier idea of "footing" in the work of

26   Limor Shifman, *Memes in Digital Culture*, Massachusetts Institute of Technology Press, 2014, p. 31.

27   Scott Atran, 'The Trouble with Memes: Conference versus Imitation in Cultural Creation," Human Nature, Springer Verlag (Germany), 2001, vol.. 12 no.. 4, p. 351–381.

28   Shifman, *Memes in Digital Culture*, p. 79.

29   Ibid., p. 170

Erving Goffman in his *Frame Analysis* (1974)[30] is perhaps the more difficult concept to grasp.

In his definitive work on the subject, John W Du Bois—writing in a compilation edited by Robert Englebretson, *Stancetaking in Discourse: Subjectivity, Evaluation, Interaction*[31]—introduces the concept of the "stance triangle", which details the evaluative and positional alignments that exist between at least two subjects and a singular object. He introduces the conclusion to his study by saying,

> Stance is not something you have, not a property of interior psyche, but something you do—something you take… Using the language of Wittgenstein, we might say: There are no private stances. We deploy overt communicative means—speech , gesture, and other forms of symbolic action—to arrive at a dialogic achievement of stance in the public arena… To realize stance dialogically means to invoke a shared framework of co-action with others.[32]

The interactivity between several subjects adopting various stances in a communicative frame does appear to describe the interpersonal process of discipleship quite well. Englebertson goes on to define stance as something a linguistic actor takes in relation to *text, linguistic codes, addressees, and other potential speakers*. Disciplers as stancetakers position themselves within their discourse directly in relation to the text of the Bible, the linguistic codes (involving such things as social indexicality), the addressees (disciples addressed individually or as a group), and toward other potential disciple-makers or influencers. For Englebertson these elements of stancetaking can be studied both quantitatively

---

30   Erving Gofman, *Frame Analysis*, Northeastern University Press, 1986.

31   Robert Englebretson, *Stancetaking in Discourse: Subjectivity, Evaluation, Interaction*, John Benjamins Publishing Company, 2007.

32   Ibid., p. 139-182.

and qualitatively, although in his opinion qualitative research renders the more substantial results.[33]

Qualitative analysis within the burgeoning subject of stance has already rendered many important insights. For instance, Alexandra Jaffe suggests that neutrality, though apparently plausible, is difficult to demonstrate as a fully discernable stance,

> Although some forms of speech and writing are more stance—saturated than others, there is no such thing is a completely neutral position vis-a-vis one's linguistic productions, because neutrality is itself a stance... By the same token, speech cannot be affectively neutral; we can indeed convey a stance of affective neutrality, but it will of necessity be read in relation to other possible emotional orientations we could have displayed.[34]

She also has some fascinating insights that might be considered in relation to contextualization. For Jaffe stance is one way to engage in contextualization,

> Goffman's concept of *footing* and Gumperz's formulation of *contextualization cues* relate to the alignments speakers take up toward themselves and others by managing the production or the reception of an utterance. At a very basic level, stance can be seen as a form of contextualization, because stancetaking indicates how the speaker's position with respect to a particular utterance or bit of text is to be interpreted; contextualization cues are thus basic, culturally specific tools or resources for stancetaking. (Italics hers)[35]

---

33   Ibid., p. 6.

34   Alexandra Jaffe, Alexandra (Ed.), *Stance: Sociolinguistic Perspectives*, Oxford University Press, 2009, p.18.

35   Ibid., p. 50.

Jaffe is suggesting that each of the orienting elements of stance points the linguistic actor in a particular direction and when taken together offer an elementary expression of contextualization.

A prominent contributor to Jaffe's compilation is Barbara Johnstone, whose research into the life and public speaking career of Barbara Jordan—a well-known Black Texan legislator of the 1960s—provides disciplers with some fascinating insights.

According to Johnson, Jordan was so influential in the legislature of the 1960s that other speakers could be described as adopting—one assumes via mimesis—the "Barbara Jordan style". This was to use a particular linguistic style that presented a "discursive enactment of epistemic and moral authority tied to ones own unique biography".[36] In other words "ethos was at the heart of Jordan's communicative style". Commenting on this use of ethos—distinct from the other classical forms of rhetoric found in logos and pathos—Johnstone states that Jordan's use of the Platonic "ethos of self " is quite different from the Aristotelian "ethos of persona", which was akin to adopting dramatic roles in a play. Jordan's self-revealing "ethos of self" led to a significant level of credibility with the audiences she addressed. Johnstone says,

> Ethos, broadly defined, is the speaker's identity as it is constructed and/or deployed in discourse…. Barbara Jordan's style of stance instantiates one of the two ways this language—ideological tradition provides for imagining the relationship between identity and discourse, and, accordingly, for imagining how rhetorical ethos works.[37]

For disciple-makers an ethos of self is vital to positioning us as credible teachers and trainers—borrowing Johnson's reference

---

36   Ibid., p. 163
37   Ibid.,161

to Quintilian's famous formulation—disciplers are "good (wo) men skilled in speaking".

An example of the compelling nature of this kind of expression of ethos is this found in the writing of John Stott. In *Between two Worlds: The Art of Preaching in the Twentieth Century*, Stott says of Dr. Billy Graham,

> I am convinced that in our day simple sincerity has not lost any of its power to appeal or to impress. It was in 1954 that Billy Graham first hit the headlines in Britain, with his Greater London Crusade. Approximately 12,000 people came to the Haringay Arena every night for three months. Most nights I was there myself, and as I looked round that vast crowd, I could not help comparing it with our half-empty churches. 'Why do these people come to listen to Billy Graham,' I asked myself, 'when they don't come to listen to us?' Now I am sure that many answers could have been justly given to that question. But the answer I kept giving myself was this: 'There is an incontrovertible sincerity about that young American evangelist. Even his fiercest critics all concede that he is sincere. I really believe he is the first transparently sincere Christian preacher many of these people have ever heard.' Today, twenty-five years later, I have found no reason to change my mind.[38]

Were the other Christian leaders that Stott had in mind less credible to their audience because they lacked depth of character, or were they simply unskilled in a presentation of an "ethos of self"? We will never know. What we can say is that ethos is an indispensable part of the discipling process and a significant element in the authentication of mimesis.

In summary we might say that although the much-contended subject of memes appears to provide little by way of concrete insight into the disciple-making process, the world

---

38   John R.W. Stott, John, *Between two Worlds: The Art of Preaching in the Twentieth Century*, Eerdmans. 1982, p. 270.

of sociolinguistics—especially where it engages the issues at the heart of mimesis and disciple-making—provides us with much to consider as we seek to develop a deeper and more comprehensive understanding of what is happening in discipling relationships.

NEGATIVE MIMESIS

As we move toward the conclusion of our chapter it is perhaps important to pause and consider whether mimesis is always an entirely positive process. Yes, ethos appears to aid the process of discipleship, but is there a time when even a presentation of a normally acceptable—even attractive—ethos does not result in the diffusion of ideas and the spiritual formation of potential disciples? One of the reasons I ask this is that my observation of leading movements of missional discipleship suggests that there may be occasions when the whole process of disciple-making produces unexpectedly negative responses among potential disciples.

René Girard, who during his lifetime was a foremost philosopher of cultural violence, suggests that mimesis—the imitation of intention and behavior—is at the very heart of violence of all kinds, especially the socially initiated violence of execution, lynching, and scapegoating. For Girard mimesis is the foundational human interaction at the heart of the development of culture. Although it is not nomenclature that Girard uses directly, he appears to differentiate between the usual "positive mimesis" of peaceful human interaction and the "negative mimesis" of the mob. Using a combination of literary anthropology and philosophical reflection, Girard demonstrates how the hidden meanings within our myths lead us to the inevitable conclusion that socially sanctioned communal violence lies at the genesis of religious systems, social hierarchies, and legal codification. With the latter he points out that the Hebrew word for "desire", which can be variously translated as envy or attraction, is translated in the 10th commandment of the Decalogue as "covet".

Covetousness is but one short step from desire, but desiring to be like someone else is the foundational impulse of the disciple toward the disciple-maker. Peter appears to represent this view when asked by Jesus whether he, like the other disciples who were offended at his teaching, would desert him. Peter replied,

> "Lord, to whom shall we go? You have the words of eternal life. We believe and know that you are the Holy One of God." (John 6:68-69)

For Girard the 10th commandment is an exposition of the motivation behind the antisocial behavior to which the laws on murder, theft, adultery and false witness all legislate.

> If the Decalogue devotes its final commandment to prohibiting desire for whatever belongs to the neighbor, it is because it lucidly recognizes in that desire the key to the violence prohibited in the four commandments that precede it. If we ceased to desire the goods of our neighbor, we would never commit murder or adultery or theft or false witness. If we respected the tenth commandment, the four commandments that precede it would be superfluous.[39]

Desire—covetousness—is the impulse behind all of these negative behaviors outlined in the second half of the Decalogue. When this impulse leads to the destructive expression of mimetic snowballing', it leads to collective violence—"violence" that is directed to the person's physical life as in murder, or to their property as with theft, or to their character as with false witness.

Armed with such insight, Girard is able to explain how apparently adoring crowds surrender to "mimetic snowballing" and become the mob that wants to lynch Christ. His satanic

---

39   Rene Girard, *I See Satan Fall Like Lightning*, Orbis Books. 2001, p.21.

antagonist incites the mob to violence subverting desire that has already been activated by Jesus the disciple-maker.

Inviting others to imitate our life is clearly vital to the disciple-making process and yet it is also something fraught with danger to the discipler. This appears to be something that Jesus warns his first disciples about,

> I am sending you out like sheep among wolves. Therefore, be as shrewd as snakes and as innocent as doves.
>
> Be on your guard against men; they will hand you over to the local councils and flog you in their synagogues.....
>
> A student is not above his teacher, nor a servant above his master. It is enough for the student to be like his teacher, and the servant like his master. If the head of the house has been called Beelzebub, how much more the members of his household! (Matthew 10:16-25)

When mimesis is subverted and redirected—either intentionally or otherwise—violence of all kinds can be the result. And yet the development of an ethos that attracts and provides a mimetic exemplar to potential disciples appears to be the inescapable and indispensable task of the disciple-maker.

CONCLUSION

As we conclude this brief excursus into the connection between preaching and disciple-making we should return to the two main areas of concern—contextualization and mimesis. As Augustine appeared to recognize in the fifth century, the skills deployed in the process of contextualization help preachers connect with potential disciples in their audience. Likewise, understanding that mimesis "is how we get to know what we know,.. (and) how we become who we are"[40] helps preachers to offer themselves and point to others as mimetic exemplars. It also prompts the use of what some would describe as memes or mimetic mnemonics; the phrases, illustrations, stories, and memorable ideas that help them communicate a message that can be lived out by their audience.

And so the connection between preaching and discipleship is not simply found in clearly communicated, contextualized information about God, the world and our personal lives, but also in the imitation of godly thought and conduct adapted and applied to the life of ordinary believers.

Preachers communicating of the gospel of Jesus Christ who want to aid in the fulfillment of the Great Commission to make disciples by their preaching would do well to become fully conversant in the skills of contextualization and mimesis. I would contend that preaching rich in these competencies could help develop ecclesial ecosystems in which discipleship naturally occurs.

---

40   McGilchrist, *The Master and Emissary*, loc. 6531 (Kindle). Edits mine.

ARC OF HISTORY & CRUCIBLE OF BIOGRAPHY

Listening is essential for contextualization. I've created the tool *Arc of History and Crucible of Biography* to give you a space for you to listen to the history of your community and the biographies of its people. Everywhere Sally and I have been sent on mission, the first thing we do is listen. In the few short months since moving to Dayton, OH, I have read a dozen books on the history of this area and city, ancient and recent, dating back to the indigenous peoples millennia before the first western settlers to the Wright Brothers to the latest events. I don't do this because I'm a bookworm, though I very well may be. We invite people into our home and listen to their stories. We do this because when we look at Jesus, Peter, Paul, and the New Testament preachers and speakers, I see that they listen before speaking.

Take the time to slow down and listen. Pay attention to the events, people, and places historically and biographically.

On the following pages, I give one additional example, this one of a middle-aged woman born in Louisiana but displaced to Dallas after Hurricane Katrina. After that, you will find a blank *Arc of History and Crucible of Biography* for you to complete.

ARC OF
HISTORY

*WHAT IS THE HISTORY
OF MY COMMUNITY?*

CRUCIBLE OF
BIOGRAPHY

*WHAT ARE THE STORIES
OF THE PEOPLE WITHIN
MY COMMUNITY?*

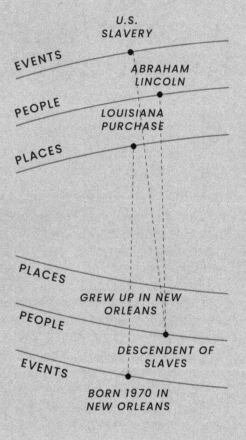

*U.S.
SLAVERY*

EVENTS

*ABRAHAM
LINCOLN*

PEOPLE

*LOUISIANA
PURCHASE*

PLACES

PLACES

*GREW UP IN NEW
ORLEANS*

PEOPLE

*DESCENDENT OF
SLAVES*

EVENTS

*BORN 1970 IN
NEW ORLEANS*

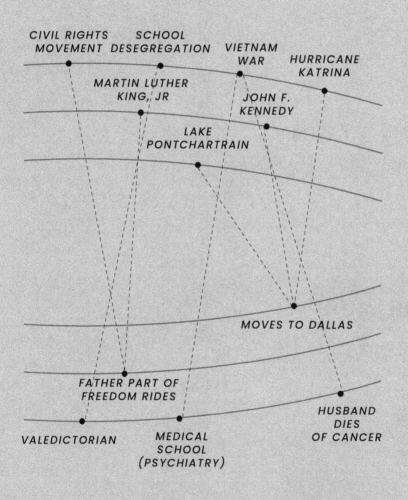

CIVIL RIGHTS   SCHOOL
MOVEMENT DESEGREGATION   VIETNAM
                              WAR   HURRICANE
                                       KATRINA

MARTIN LUTHER
KING, JR   JOHN F.
                      KENNEDY

LAKE
PONTCHARTRAIN

MOVES TO DALLAS

FATHER PART OF
FREEDOM RIDES
                              HUSBAND
                              DIES
VALEDICTORIAN   MEDICAL   OF CANCER
                  SCHOOL
                  (PSYCHIATRY)

ARC OF
HISTORY

WHAT IS THE HISTORY
OF MY COMMUNITY?

EVENTS

PEOPLE

PLACES

CRUCIBLE OF
BIOGRAPHY

WHAT ARE THE STORIES
OF THE PEOPLE WITHIN
MY COMMUNITY?

PLACES

PEOPLE

EVENTS

BIBLIOGRAPHY

Atran, S, "The Trouble with Memes: Conference Versus Imitation in Cultural Creation," *Human Nature*, Springer Verlag (Germany), 2001 vol. 12 no. 4, pp. 351 – 381.

Aunger, Robert, *The Electric Meme: A New Theory of How we Think*, 2002, New York: Simon & Schuster.

C. Beard. "Missional Discipleship: Discerning spiritual-information practices and goals within the missional movement," *Missiology: An International Review* 2015, vol. 43(2) pp. 175–194.

Blackmore, Susan, *The Meme Machine*, 1999, Oxford: Oxford University Press.

Breen, M., *Growing the Smaller Church*, 1991, London: CPAS.

: *Building a Discipling Culture,* 3rd ed., 2017, 3DM Publishing.

: *Covenant and Kingdom: The DNA of the Bible*, 2010, 3DM Publishing.

: *Leading Kingdom Movements*, 2013, 3DM Publishing.

Breen, Mike and Sally, *Family on Mission*, 2nd ed., 2015, 3DM Publishing.

Brodie, Richard, *Virus of the Mind: The New Science of the Meme*, 1999, Integral Press.

Dawkins, Richard, *The Selfish Gene*, 1989, Oxford University Press.

Distin, Kate, *The Selfish Meme: A Critical Reassessment*, 2005, Cambridge University Press.

Englebertson, Robert, *Stancetaking in Discourse: Subjectivity, Evaluation, Interaction*, 2007, John Benjamins Publishing Company.

Gatherer, Derek, "Why is the 'Thought Contagion' Metaphor is Retarding the Progress of Memetics?" School of Biomolecular Sciences Liverpool, John Moores University.

Girard, Rene, *See Satan Fall Like Lightning,* 2001, Maryknoll, NY: Orbis.

Gofman, E. *Frame Analysis*, 1986, Northeastern University Press.,

Guder, Darrell L., *The Continuing Conversion of the Church*, 2000, Grand Rapids, MI: Eerdmans.

Halter, Hugh and Smay, Matt, *And: The Gathered and Scattered Church,* 2010, Zonderzan.

Jaffe, Alexandra (Ed.), *Stance: Sociolinguistic Perspectives,* 2009, Oxford University Press.

Johnstone, Barbara, "Stance, Style, and the Linguistic Individual' in *Stance—Sociolinguistic Perspectives* edited by Alexandra Jaffe, 2009, Oxford University Press.

McGilchrist, I. *The Master and his Emissary—The Divided Brain and the Making of the Western World.*, 2009, London: Yale University Press.

: *The Divided Brain and the Search for Meaning (Why Are We So Unhappy?)*, 2012, Yale University Press.

Miller, Donald, *A Million Miles in a Thousand Years*, 2009, Nashville, TN: Thomas Nelson.

Mills, C. Wright, *The Sociological Imagination*, 1959, Oxford: Oxford University Press.

Ramachandran, V.S. "Mirror Neurons and Imitation Learning as the Driving Force Behind 'The Great Leap Forward' in Human Evolution," from *The Third Culture*: http:// www. edge.org/3rd_culture/.

Ramsey, Ian, *Models and Mystery*, 1964, Oxford University Press.

Richerson, Peter and Boyd, Robert *Culture and Evolutionary Process,* 1985, Chicago: The University of Chicago Press.

Sachs, Jonah, *Winning the Story Wars*, 2012, Boston, MA: Harvard Business School Publishing.

: *Not by Genes Alone, How Culture Transformed Human Evolution*, 2005, University of Chicago Press.

Shifman, Limor, *Memes in Digital* Culture, 2014, Massachusetts Institute of Technology Press.

: "Memes in a Digital World: Reconciling with a Conceptual Troublemaker," *Journal of Computational Mediated Communication*, 2013, vol. 18, no.3 pp. 362-377.

: "An Anatomy of a YouTube Meme," *New Media Society* 2012, vol 14 (2) pp. 187 – 203.

Smith, Christian, et. al., *Lost in Translation*, 2011, Oxford: Oxford University Press.

Stark, Rodney, *The Rise of Christianity*, 1997, Princeton, NJ: Princeton University Press.

Stott, John R.W. *Between Two Worlds: The Art of Preaching in the Twentieth Century*, 1982, Grand Rapids: Eerdmans.

Thiselton, Anthony, *The Two Horizons*, 1980, Grand Rapids, MI: Eerdmans.

Vanhoozer, Kevin, *Everyday Theology*, 2007, Grand Rapids, MI: Baker Academic.

Vogler, Christopher, T*he Writer's Journey: Mythic Structure for Writers*, 3rd ed., 2007, Studio City, CA: Michael Weis Productions.

Wilkins, Michael, *Following the Master: A Biblical Theology of Discipleship*, 1992, Grand Rapids, MI: Zondervan.

ISBN 978-1-945455-01-8

90000